AF848957

SOCIAL JUSTICE, EQUALITY AND EMPOWERMENT

HUMAN TRAFFICKING IN EUROPE AND EURASIA: PREVENTION, PROTECTION AND VICTIM ASSISTANCE

Social Justice, Equality and Empowerment

Additional books in this series can be found on Nova's website under the Series tab.

Additional E-books in this series can be found on Nova's website under the E-books tab.

Law, Crime and Law Enforcement

Additional books in this series can be found on Nova's website under the Series tab.

Additional E-books in this series can be found on Nova's website under the E-books tab.

SOCIAL JUSTICE, EQUALITY AND EMPOWERMENT

HUMAN TRAFFICKING IN EUROPE AND EURASIA: PREVENTION, PROTECTION AND VICTIM ASSISTANCE

CHARLES R. SCOTT
AND
ALEXANDER D. CHASE
EDITORS

Nova Science Publishers, Inc.
New York

Copyright © 2011 by Nova Science Publishers, Inc.

All rights reserved. No part of this book may be reproduced, stored in a retrieval system or transmitted in any form or by any means: electronic, electrostatic, magnetic, tape, mechanical photocopying, recording or otherwise without the written permission of the Publisher.

For permission to use material from this book please contact us:
Telephone 631-231-7269; Fax 631-231-8175
Web Site: http://www.novapublishers.com

NOTICE TO THE READER

The Publisher has taken reasonable care in the preparation of this book, but makes no expressed or implied warranty of any kind and assumes no responsibility for any errors or omissions. No liability is assumed for incidental or consequential damages in connection with or arising out of information contained in this book. The Publisher shall not be liable for any special, consequential, or exemplary damages resulting, in whole or in part, from the readers' use of, or reliance upon, this material. Any parts of this book based on government reports are so indicated and copyright is claimed for those parts to the extent applicable to compilations of such works.

Independent verification should be sought for any data, advice or recommendations contained in this book. In addition, no responsibility is assumed by the publisher for any injury and/or damage to persons or property arising from any methods, products, instructions, ideas or otherwise contained in this publication.

This publication is designed to provide accurate and authoritative information with regard to the subject matter covered herein. It is sold with the clear understanding that the Publisher is not engaged in rendering legal or any other professional services. If legal or any other expert assistance is required, the services of a competent person should be sought. FROM A DECLARATION OF PARTICIPANTS JOINTLY ADOPTED BY A COMMITTEE OF THE AMERICAN BAR ASSOCIATION AND A COMMITTEE OF PUBLISHERS.

Additional color graphics may be available in the e-book version of this book.

LIBRARY OF CONGRESS CATALOGING-IN-PUBLICATION DATA

Human trafficking in Europe and Eurasia : prevention, protection, and victim
assistance / editors, Charles R. Scott and Alexander D. Chase.
p. cm.
Includes index.
ISBN 978-1-61122-913-4 (hardcover)
1. Human trafficking--Europe, Eastern. 2. Human trafficking--Europe,
Central. 3. Human trafficking--Prevention--International cooperation. I.
Scott, Charles R. II. Chase, Alexander D. III. United States. Agency for
International Development.
HQ281.H8686 2011
364.15--dc22
2010047015

Published by Nova Science Publishers, Inc. † New York

CONTENTS

PREFACE

This book examines practices in activities designed to prevent trafficking in persons (TIP) in the countries of the European and Eurasian regions. This book provides an analytical review of interventions aimed at identifying and assisting victims. Protection projects include a wide range of interventions, from building the capacity of government and civil society stakeholders to the development and provision of services to victims, establishing appropriate legislation, regulations and policies.

Chapter 1- This chapter was commissioned by USAID's Europe & Eurasia (E&E) Bureau to examine best practices in activities designed to prevent trafficking in persons (TIP) in the countries of the E&E region. The purpose of this chapter is to assist the E&E Bureau to improve anti-trafficking in persons programs in terms of effectiveness and impact, thereby reducing the incidence of TIP. USAID seeks to determine the strengths and weaknesses of program approaches to date and discover where anti-TIP efforts can be integrated into other relevant USAID programming.

Chapter 2- The report that follows is an assessment of trafficking protection programs – programs designed to provide protection and assistance to victims of trafficking. It is intended to help USAID and other interested parties determine the strengths and weaknesses of program approaches to date, ascertain which projects are replicable and where anti-TIP efforts can be integrated into other relevant USAID programming. A companion report has been written to assess trafficking prevention programs.

In: Human Trafficking in Europe and… ISBN: 978-1-61122-913-4
Editors: Charles R. Scott et al. © 2011 Nova Science Publishers, Inc.

Chapter 1

BEST PRACTICES IN TRAFFICKING PREVENTION IN EUROPE & EURASIA[*]

United States Agency for International Development

ACKNOWLEDGMENTS

This study was possible because of the commitment of USAID's Europe and Eurasia Bureau to support research designed to improve responses by the United States and other countries to trafficking in persons. Several individuals at USAID in particular need to be acknowledged. I would like to thank Catherine Cozzarelli of USAID's Europe and Eurasia Bureau for her leadership and support on this research. Before she departed USAID, Ruth Pojman, who now works on the issue of human trafficking for the Organization for Security and Cooperation in Europe, provided material and input for which I am very appreciative. Glenn Rogers is to be commended for having the vision to recognize the importance of investing in research to inform and improve the practices of anti-trafficking work in the region. In the E&E region there are many people working in the USAID missions who care deeply about this issue, and this research reflects their desire to address it more effectively.

---

[*] This is an edited, reformatted and augmented edition of a United States Agency For International Development publication, dated January 2009.

Creative Associates International and the Aguirre Division of JBS International, Inc. provided the opportunity to conduct this research. Throughout this process, I received much appreciated support and input from Deepika Chawla and Sylvia Ellison of Creative Associates and Christine Allison of Aguirre. They have been a pleasure to work with throughout this process.

Ruth Rosenberg wrote the companion report to this one ("Best Practices for Programming to Protect and Assist Victims of Trafficking in Europe and Eurasia"). Ruth is an accomplished researcher and has contributed much toward understanding the issue of trafficking in persons and the responses to it. I am pleased to have had a chance to work with her.

At the NEXUS Institute, I am fortunate to work with Rebecca Surtees. As Senior Researcher at NEXUS, Rebecca has completed as much research on the issue of human trafficking in this region as anyone, especially primary research based on the perspectives and experiences of victims of trafficking. This chapter, which relies upon portions of that body of work, reflects Rebecca's findings.

Finally, I would like to thank all who have supported the NEXUS Institute and our work to improve laws, policies, and practice to combat human trafficking around the world.

Stephen Warnath
Executive Director
NEXUS Institute

EXECUTIVE SUMMARY

This chapter was commissioned by USAID's Europe & Eurasia (E&E) Bureau to examine best practices in activities designed to prevent trafficking in persons (TIP) in the countries of the E&E region. The purpose of this chapter is to assist the E&E Bureau to improve anti-trafficking in persons programs in terms of effectiveness and impact, thereby reducing the incidence of TIP. USAID seeks to determine the strengths and weaknesses of program approaches to date and discover where anti-TIP efforts can be integrated into other relevant USAID programming.

To achieve this goal, this chapter highlights TIP best practices and lessons learned that were extracted from the available project-specific literature, primarily documents produced in conjunction with USAID-supported projects and supplemented by a larger review of the literature relevant to anti-trafficking prevention strategies and methods. (A complete listing of sources is found in Annex A: References.) This chapter builds upon the work of a 2004 assessment entitled "Best Practices to Prevent Trafficking in Persons in Europe and Eurasia" by Ruth Rosenberg.[1] A companion report ("Best Practices for Programming to Protect and Assist Victims of Trafficking in Europe and Eurasia") reviews protection and assistance programs for TIP victims in the E&E region.

This chapter covers the following countries: Albania, Armenia, Azerbaijan, Belarus, Bosnia and Herzegovina (BiH), Bulgaria, Croatia, Cyprus, Georgia, Kazakhstan, Kosovo, Kyrgyzstan, the Republic of Macedonia, Moldova, Montenegro, Romania, Russia, Serbia, Tajikistan, Turkmenistan, Ukraine, and Uzbekistan.[2]

Methodology & Limitations

The literature reviewed in preparation for this chapter was extensive, including a review of international governmental and non-governmental reports, newspaper articles, and academic publications. Publications and websites of USAID and other U.S. Government agencies, as well as their implementing partners, were searched for applicable material. The websites of a number of NGO service providers and international organizations, including those based or working in the region, were reviewed. Finally, the global resource center on anti-trafficking issues at the NEXUS Institute was utilized. This library and resource center contains over 2,000 counter-trafficking documents, among them project descriptions; research reports and studies; relevant laws, policies and programs; and articles on trafficking and anti-trafficking work, including many published by NGO service providers located in the E&E region.

Despite the extensive literature review, this chapter was necessarily limited in time and scope. No field research was undertaken, and limited budgetary resources permitted no first-hand verification of the data presented in the literature. Further, the lack of project evaluations hinders the author's ability to compare the efficacy of TIP prevention activities or to identify "best practices" in any way other than preliminary. Gaps in the coverage of TIP in the E&E literature also exist, and there are few programs designed to prevent certain forms of trafficking (e.g., labor trafficking).

Analysis of Prevention Programs

In general, prevention activities may be understood to include any intervention aimed at reducing or eliminating the likelihood of human trafficking and re-trafficking. Prevention programs are typically divided into four categories:

- Changing the overall context or environment (social, cultural, economic, political/legal) in which TIP occurs;
- Addressing one or more variables associated with an individual (a "potential victim") that may contribute to a heightened risk or vulnerability (e.g., lack of information, family crisis, economic problems);
- Targeting the criminals and establishing deterrence in the form of an effective justice system; and
- Increasing the ability of officials and others to identify potential TIP cases prior to the occurrence of TIP exploitation and to enable appropriate intervention (e.g., at border crossings).

In order to more thoroughly understand prevention programs, it is useful to analyze them within the more specific subcategories of awareness raising, employment, income-generation, empowerment, crisis prevention and violence mitigation, safe migration, demand reduction, protection as prevention, and deterrence through criminalization. Various prevention programs may fall under multiple categories and activities, or methods utilized within categories may serve multiple purposes.

In each of these areas, USAID Missions and other donors have funded programs, the vast majority of which use awareness raising, employment, and empowerment activities as the anchors of their efforts. Examples of prevention initiatives implemented by TIP prevention projects in the E&E region are presented in the body of this chapter. The outcomes of TIP prevention projects have been successful by some measures – potential victims of trafficking (VoTs) are more aware of situations from which they could be trafficked, and in many countries where awareness campaigns have been conducted the general population is more aware of the existence and risks of TIP. The evidence for success in other kinds of prevention programs, however, and of long-term TIP prevention is rarely available.

Conclusions

Building upon prevention efforts initiated approximately ten years ago, USAID projects have grown significantly in reach and breadth in countries of the E&E region. Reports document a number of positive changes in attitudes and behaviors in the lives of many participants in anti-TIP programs. Determining the effectiveness of prevention programs, however, has remained problematic. It is not possible, at least based upon a document review, to assess comparative effectiveness of specific programs or approaches to reducing TIP in the region.

The context of risk and vulnerability in which TIP flourishes – and that prevention work seeks to alter – is complicated. The breadth, pervasiveness, and in many cases intransigience of factors contributing to the existence of TIP present a serious test for all prevention activities. Unfortunately, the design and implementation of TIP prevention initiatives rarely address this complexity. And because so little empirical work has been done regarding these factors, many assumptions have emerged to fill the void.

Accordingly, the key challenge for improving prevention efforts is two-fold: 1) insufficient data on the root causes, contributing factors, vulnerabilities, and risks that may lead to TIP in general and to the diverse manifestations of TIP in different countries and communities; and 2) insufficient data on the prevention of trafficking as a result of TIP prevention programming. Improvement in prevention results should follow from increasing this understanding and from testing the current assumptions about the relationship between activity and outcomes upon which prevention measures rest.

Recommendations

The full analysis and discussion that form the basis of the recommendations presented comprise the main body of this chapter.

1. Donors and TIP prevention program implementers should **strengthen the understanding of underlying contributing factors in order to improve TIP prevention programming.**
   a. Analyze what type of data needs to be collected – and how it can be collected across the region – to form the basis of reliable

empirical findings about root causes, contributing factors, risks, and vulnerabilities linked to TIP.

b. Ascertain what factors work to counter vulnerabilities and risk of potential victims of TIP. Analyze what differentiates the circumstances of similarly situated individuals, some who are eventually trafficked and some who are not.

2. Donors and TIP prevention program implementers should **refine the link between project activities and TIP prevention outcomes.**
   a. Gather new data for prevention results assessments.
   b. Develop long term frameworks within which individual TIP projects are located to permit determination of prevention results. Strategies should be developed, including post-project evaluation methods, to compensate for existing structural impediments (e.g., short-term, incremental projects).
   c. Incorporate into future TIP projects data collection procedures that will permit evaluation by independent evaluators and researchers at points in time after the completion of the project.
   d. Design research projects to answer questions specific to establishing the link between TIP prevention activities and prevention results.
   e. Require monitoring and evaluation (M&E) to be an integral component of TIP prevention projects.
   f. Develop baselines and outcome indicators that are specific, meaningful, and measurable.
   g. Utilize impact evaluations to illustrate positive and negative results as well as intended and unintended consequences.
   h. Fund the budget requirements for projects to implement sound M&E.
   i. Develop incentives for TIP prevention project applicants and/or implementers to initiate stronger outcome indicators for their respective projects to supplement and link to output measures.
   j. Supplement internal evaluation of TIP prevention projects with external evaluation work. Self-evaluation by project implementers, although useful for project management purposes and for donors as part of a larger evaluation approach, is not a substitute for objective assessments by experienced researchers and evaluators.

3. Donors and TIP prevention program implementing organizations should work together to **refine their ability to target prevention programs to at-risk groups.**
   a. With more precision, identify and disaggregate groups at risk of being potential victims of TIP.
   b. Address all forms of trafficking in persons in implementation of TIP prevention strategies.
   c. Identify all populations underserved by TIP prevention projects for each country in the E&E region.
   d. Incorporate neglected at-risk groups into TIP prevention strategy development and program design. Strategies and projects should be adapted for and tailored to these groups in order to achieve maximum effectiveness.
   e. Extend TIP prevention efforts more systematically to reach at-risk populations in rural communities.
   f. Examine opportunities to partner/collaborate with prevention-related projects provided by governments and NGOs, especially to expand ability to reach underserved populations and/or communities with TIP prevention efforts.
4. Donors and TIP prevention program implementing organizations should **prioritize TIP awareness-raising projects that emphasize prevention.**
   a. For projects in countries reporting extremely high levels of TIP awareness (i.e., awareness saturation) among their populations, examine whether adjustments should be undertaken to improve prevention effectiveness rather than continuing the status quo of message saturation.
   b. Emphasize TIP awareness projects that demonstrate over time prevention results instead of information "campaigns" with general messages (with the exception of outreach to areas that still have little prior knowledge of TIP).
   c. Avoid sensationalized, alarmist, or frightening awareness messages. Scare tactics about TIP do not appear to resonate with intended recipients of those messages.
   d. Examine whether messages that provide ways for the individuals to protect themselves from falling victims to TIP lead to better prevention results than general messages.

e. Determine more precisely how different groups take in, process, digest, and act upon messages. Generic messages have dubious prevention value.
f. Magnify the impact of awareness/prevention messages by tailoring them more precisely to narrowly targeted audiences.
g. Test prevention messages for effectiveness with minors of different age-groups. Assume that anti-TIP messages created for adults will not resonate effectively with children.
h. Revisit awareness messages for men; consider specifically whether adjustments are necessary due to resistance to the "victim" label for VoTs.
i. Consider whether experts in advertising and media message content can contribute to the development of awareness messages and strategies by TIP prevention projects.
j. Examine whether there are lessons to be learned from those experienced with awareness campaigns designed to change behavior or attitudes for issues such as domestic violence or HIV/AIDS.
k. To the extent appropriate and ethical, seek to include participation of former VoTs to elicit their first-hand perspectives in the design of TIP prevention projects.

5. Donors and TIP prevention program implementing organizations should **tighten the link between employment-based, income-generating, and empowerment prevention activities and long-term prevention results.**
   a. Monitor job placement over time for graduates of economic-based courses. If necessary, continue documenting beyond initial job placement to evaluate prevention impact associated with sustained local employment. Only over time (at least one year after the conclusion of the project) can prevention results be assessed.
   b. Examine the effectiveness of achieving TIP prevention arising from skills training and empowerment programs within the context of local employment and economic conditions in each country of the E&E region. Review, for example, the extent to which graduates of these programs from economically suppressed areas ultimately migrate to other countries seeking employment and what happens to graduates who stay but do not find jobs.

   c. Conduct further research regarding tailoring the design of income-generating projects to serve TIP prevention objectives most effectively.

6. Donors and TIP prevention program implementing organizations should **ensure that safe migration projects supported by anti-TIP grants and contracts are tailored specifically to maximize the achievement of TIP prevention objectives.**
   a. Data gathering and analysis of safe migration TIP prevention projects need to be strengthened to begin to identify factors and circumstances (apart from the criminal intervention of a trafficker) of program participants that differentiate an individual who migrates successfully from one who is trafficked. To start, data should be collected from assisted VoTs about whether they participated in safe migration projects prior to being trafficked and why, from their perspective, the content of those projects failed to prevent them from being trafficked.
   b. Examine whether cooperative partnerships can be developed between NGOs in countries of origin and those in countries of destination in order to vet jobs in destination countries. Consideration could also be given to whether job vetting is a prevention approach for which government-NGO collaborations could be developed.
7. Donors and TIP prevention program implementing organizations should **include demand reduction approaches** that demonstrate effective TIP prevention results as part of comprehensive TIP prevention strategy.
   a. Address demand reduction as part of comprehensive TIP prevention strategies.
   b. Conduct the first analysis of the effectiveness of demand as a prevention method for different forms of TIP.
8. Donors and TIP prevention program implementing organizations should **consider TIP prevention impact of gender-based factors.**
   a. Determine if gender stereotypes about who is likely to be a TIP victim and preconceptions hamper TIP prevention efforts.

PURPOSE AND METHODOLOGY

Purpose

The purpose of this chapter is to assist the Europe & Eurasia (E&E) Bureau to improve the effectiveness of programs to prevent and reduce trafficking in persons (TIP). Toward this goal, this chapter highlights selected TIP "best practices" and lessons learned that were extracted from written studies and reports. This chapter also identifies several fundamental obstacles impeding the E&E Bureau's ability to determine, evaluate, and compare the quality of prevention results and the prevention effectiveness of its projects.

An initial assessment of USAID anti-trafficking prevention programs in the E&E region was conducted in 2004 by Ruth Rosenberg, "Best Practices for Programming to Prevent Trafficking in Human Beings in Europe and Eurasia" (2004). This paper extends the findings of Rosenberg's article and provides additional insights to improve the impact and cost effectiveness of prevention projects in the region.

This chapter is not intended to be a "how-to" manual on prevention for practitioners, nor is it within the scope of this chapter to catalog and describe all prevention projects supported by USAID or others in the region. Given the breadth of activities included in many of the projects, such an exercise would easily overwhelm the central purpose (and intended scope) of this chapter, which is to consider ways to advance the effectiveness of future prevention efforts. Further, more detailed and updated information about projects than is possible to include here is available from many of the projects' websites, project informational brochures, and other public sources. Moreover, many of the specific project numbers reviewed for this chapter will be superseded by newer data by the time this chapter is published. Rather than focus on numbers, this chapter attempts to derive insights and lessons that will broaden the usefulness of available data. Finally, as indicated above, this chapter is intended to build upon, and not retread, ground covered by Rosenberg's earlier report that provides an excellent introduction to the nature of prevention efforts generally and prevention projects specifically through 2004 in the E&E region.

Rosenberg's report describes the range of prevention approaches applied in the E&E region. It finds that prevention efforts in the region have had success in preventing the trafficking of individuals, although documentation of these successes is mostly anecdotal. The study also finds that the general population was more aware of trafficking and the exploitation of migrants than it had been prior to TIP prevention programs. Aside from these successes, however, the study reveals that TIP prevention programs may have driven traffickers to change their methods of operation, either in recruitment, transit routes, or secrecy of operations.

It is hoped that this chapter may serve donors who are developing and funding prevention projects to improve those projects in the future.

Methodology

This chapter takes the current literature about prevention projects in the E&E region as a starting point to examine prevention interventions and the extent to which they have prevented human trafficking.

The literature reviewed in preparation for this chapter was extensive. It included international governmental and non-governmental reports, newspaper articles, and academic publications. To aid this endeavor, the E&E Bureau provided over one hundred project reports and related documents from its files. Publications and websites of USAID and other U.S. Government agencies, as well as their contracting firms, were searched for applicable material. The websites of a number of NGO service providers and international organizations, including those based or working in the region, were reviewed. Finally, the global resource center on anti-trafficking issues at the NEXUS Institute was utilized. This library and resource center contains over 2,000 counter-trafficking documents, among them project descriptions; research reports and studies; relevant laws, policies and programs; and articles on trafficking and anti-trafficking work, including many published by NGO service providers located in the E&E region.

Limitations

The preparation of this chapter was necessarily limited by a number of factors. First, as a short-term literature review, the research project was limited in time and scope. No field research was undertaken, and limited budgetary resources permitted no first-hand verification of the data presented in the literature. Furthermore, while many documents describe project activities, relatively few address project evaluations. Projects provide many output numbers but few outcome or results numbers. Where prevention projects show gaps in types of trafficking (e.g., labor trafficking), there are gaps in information.

ANALYSIS OF PREVENTION PROGRAMS

In general, prevention activities may be understood to include any intervention aimed at reducing or eliminating the likelihood of human trafficking and re-trafficking. Prevention programs are typically divided into four categories:

- Changing the overall context or environment (social, cultural, economic, political/legal) in which TIP occurs;
- Addressing one or more variables associated with an individual (i.e., a "potential victim") that may contribute to a heightened risk or vulnerability (e.g., lack of information, family crisis, economic problems);
- Targeting the criminals and establishing deterrence in the form of an effective justice system; and
- Increasing the ability of officials and others to identify potential TIP cases prior to the occurrence of the TIP exploitation and to enable these individuals to intervene appropriately (e.g., at border crossings).

The United States' support for TIP prevention programs in the E&E region is not new. The United States Agency for International Development (USAID) as well as other U.S. Government entities – notably the U.S. Department of State's Office of the Undersecretary of State for Global Affairs[3], its Bureau of Population, Refugees, and Migration, and the United States Information Agency[4]– initiated such anti-trafficking projects over a decade ago. These prevention efforts combined awareness raising and economic opportunity initiatives.

Building upon this decade-long experience of implementing prevention activities in the E&E region, USAID has continued to increase the scope of its prevention strategies as well as to expand prevention activities to additional E&E countries. A partial list of on-going and past USAID-supported projects directed at preventing TIP in whole or in part includes:

- Albania: The Coordinated Action Against Human Trafficking (CAAHT) program, implemented by Creative Associates (2004-2009), is a comprehensive approach to anti-TIP programming engaging civil society and government. The primary activity strengthens the capacity and participation of civil society for trafficking prevention and supports assistance for and the reintegration of trafficking victims. As part of wide-ranging activities directed at the prevention of child trafficking, the Transnational Action against Child Trafficking (TACT) program, implemented by Terre des Hommes (TdH) (2006-2010), focuses on the identification of at-risk children and conducting related prevention activities.
- Croatia: USAID prevention efforts included support for NGOs in selected border communities to raise awareness and public understanding of the risks of trafficking in their localities and to provide the public with information on where to turn when they detect cases of trafficking (implemented by World Learning, 2004-2006). The USAID Mission, with the Ministry of Education, developed awareness material for use in schools (implemented by the IOM, 2002-2003).
- Central Asian Republics (CAR): USAID has supported far-ranging prevention initiatives in CAR. This included:
  - Kyrgyz Republic: USAID provided support for 18 local NGOs implementing prevention activities in the Preventing Human Trafficking Project in Kyrgyzstan (Winrock International, 2003-2005).
  - Kazakhstan: USAID supported awareness raising among vulnerable groups; job skills training; crisis centers; shelters; and training for religious leaders, medical professionals and educators (implemented by IOM, n.d.).
  - Tajikistan: USAID supported work of the IOM in Tajikistan to develop an anti-trafficking information campaign.
  - Uzbekistan: USAID supports IOM's anti-trafficking activities, which include broad awareness and prevention efforts.
- Georgia: USAID's program supported sweeping prevention activities using IRIS/Georgia and the Georgian Young Lawyers Association (2005-2008). These activities focused on trafficking prevention by working with students in schools and by public events and outreach campaigns to reach the general population.

- Kosovo: Among its activities, USAID has supported informational and awareness-raising activities.
- Moldova: Efforts have focused especially on the economic roots of trafficking and improving access to employment within Moldova for young women and girls. Activities include: awareness raising; victim assistance and support services; outreach; and development of employment/business opportunities.
- Montenegro: USAID funded IOM's public information activities targeting actual and potential TIP victims and local populations in areas most at risk for trafficking.
- Romania: USAID/Romania supported NGOs to implement activities aimed at preventing vulnerable children, especially street children, from becoming victims of trafficking (VoTs). Activities included life skills training and social/occupational services for children who left state welfare institutions.
- Russia: Efforts included support for the ambitious Path to Success program to inform and educate youth and their families in the Russian Far East about the dangers of human trafficking (implemented by Winrock International, 2003-2008). The program supported two grants for NGOs. One grant raised public awareness to reinforce anti-trafficking messages and positive values needed to address the underlying causes of trafficking. The second established NGO-teacher partnerships to train teachers to integrate life skills, leadership, and self-esteem building topics to increase economic alternatives for young women. In other parts of Russia, USAID supported training in leadership, job and entrepreneurial skills, and the creation of NGO networks to increase public awareness of human trafficking and to develop practical employment alternatives for women and girls (implemented by IREX, 2001-2004).
- Serbia: USAID funded the IOM (2002-2005) to conduct, in cooperation with a local NGO (Beosupport), an anti-trafficking awareness-raising campaign throughout Serbia. In addition, the Regional Clearing Point, based in Belgrade, undertook the most comprehensive collection and analysis of national and regional trafficking data (including trafficking patterns, recruitment practices, routes and profile data on victims assisted) and the assistance and protection programs existing in the region for trafficking victims (Surtees, 2005).

- Ukraine: USAID has supported large scale projects in Ukraine, one led by IOM (2004-2009) and another that was previously headed by Winrock International (1998-2004). Together, the projects have provided Ukraine with an extensive range of prevention activities across the country, including working intensively with women and children to utilize a number of support and empowerment methods such as walk-in services and training in job search strategies and business development. Other activities involve increasing awareness among government and community leaders, service providers, and the general public.

The foregoing overview is only a partial indication of the commitment that USAID has made to prevention efforts across the E&E region.

In order to more thoroughly understand prevention programs, it is useful to analyze them within the more specific subcategories of awareness raising, employment, income-generation, empowerment, crisis prevention/violence mitigation, safe migration, demand reduction, protection as prevention, and crime prevention/enforcement as TIP deterence.[5] Various prevention programs may fall under multiple categories, and activities or methods utilized within categories may serve multiple purposes.

Raising Awareness

Awareness as a prevention tool is based on the premise that information can help individuals anticipate, recognize, and avoid the many ways that traffickers use deception or coercion against them. In several respects, awareness serves as a foundation upon which other elements of a successful anti-trafficking strategy are built. Without first establishing a minimum level of understanding of human trafficking, it is impossible to identify VoTs, provide assistance, or to garner the political will needed to combat TIP.

The literature reviewed for this chapter describes a variety of awareness-raising approaches that have been utilized in the E&E region, including the following:

1. Operating helplines and hotlines to disseminate information;
2. Putting on trafficking awareness events such as concerts, theater productions, street performances, art exhibits, parades, and dances;

3. Developing and broadcasting television public service announcements (PSAs);
4. Hosting or creating radio and television programs;
5. Developing soap operas or other televised dramatic depictions;
6. Creating and showing documentary films;
7. Publishing and disseminating brochures, posters, flyers, and other printed material;
8. Placing billboards and/or informational materials on public transportation;
9. Distributing anti-trafficking messages on "give-aways" such as t-shirts, pens, bags, or notebooks;
10. Conducting training seminars for specific target audiences such as government officials, law enforcement, journalists, students, teachers, and medical practitioners;
11. Working with religious leaders and institutions on outreach;
12. Carrying out empowerment programs (with an awareness component);
13. Holding conferences, dialogues, lectures, exchanges, town meetings, discussion groups, or roundtables;
14. Running summer camps for youth;
15. Preparing curricula for use in schools and training of teachers in the curriculum as well as developing after-school programs and parent-student dialogues;
16. Sponsoring essay and drawing contests and debates for students;
17. Creating cartoons to reach children; and
18. Placing trafficking awareness advertisements or PSAs in newspapers and magazines.[6]

Without question, anti-trafficking organizations in the region have applied a broad and creative array of vehicles to distribute information about TIP to a variety of populations.

The purpose of awareness raising can vary. When the awareness raising involves trafficking prevention, the messages typically attempt to educate individuals about the risks and dangers of human trafficking in ways that enhance decision making and action taking in order to lower the risk of being trafficked. Awareness-raising activities, however, can also serve objectives other than prevention. For example, activities may involve distributing basic information to introduce and educate readers about the existence of the phenomenon. Or awareness-raising activities may impart information about how to identify and report a suspected case of human trafficking. Some awareness-raising campaigns are focused on advocacy and directed toward policymakers (e.g., they convey the message that trafficking is an international human rights issue or that an anti-trafficking law is needed). Other awareness raising seeks to change attitudes about VoTs to decrease stereotypes and stigma.[7]

USAID and other donors have supported a number of large awareness programs in the E&E region. Contrasted with the earliest projects in the late 1990s, current projects have grown significantly in size and scope. Moreover, whereas the awareness-raising efforts of those original projects were primarily "paper-based," utilizing media such as posters, pamphlets, and flyers, efforts now involve more holistic and multi-faceted awareness campaigns that utilize multiple approaches.

In Georgia, for example, an awareness project implemented for USAID by the Georgia Young Lawyers Association (GYLA)[8] employed a range of awareness methods with multiple target groups to increase knowledge of the risk of trafficking. Working with the Ministry of Education and Science and anti-trafficking experts, the GYLA conducted awareness-raising campaigns in schools. The anti-trafficking meetings held at dozens of schools were attended by nearly 900 children and 40 teachers. At the end of these meetings, awareness-raising materials – postcards, bookmarks, pens, and notebooks – were distributed to reinforce the message. At the conclusion of the school year, GYLA continued awareness raisings for youth on TIP issues by turning its attention to boarding schools, where homeless children or children with disabilities live and study.

To expand its reach, GYLA collaborated with an organization that holds free concerts for youth on public holidays, encouraging singers to address concert-going youth with anti-trafficking messages and to wear anti-trafficking t-shirts. GYLA also organized meetings, attended by up to 400 people, intended to educate the general population on human trafficking. Other awareness-raising activities for the general population included the following:

- T-shirts with the project's message were distributed.
- Call-in radio shows, television talk shows, a documentary, and PSAs on radio broadcasts were conducted.
- Small stands holding awareness booklets were strategically placed around Georgia, for example, in embassies, consulates and international organizations, Ministry of Education Resource Centers, international organizations, and NGOs.

- Anti-TIP campaign stickers were widely displayed in the Tbilisi subway and in buses in Georgian cities.
- A joint working group was created by NGOs and international organizations for sharing information to avoid duplication and to maximize resources for awareness raising and other activities in the country.

These activities suggest the sweeping nature of this effort—national in scope, with multiple target groups and a range of mobilized mediums and methods. Other ambitious awareness campaigns supported by USAID were implemented in Ukraine, Moldova, Russia, Albania, and the countries of the Central Asia Region. The scale of awareness activities of some projects appears to be based upon a saturation strategy, its primary objective to blanket a country's residents with anti-trafficking messages. In their reports to USAID, project implementers have documented prodigiously the outputs of such awareness-raising activities. The sheer output for projects in a number of the countries has been immense.

Smaller scale awareness-raising projects have been conducted in other countries in the E&E region as well. At the same time, other donors and organizations have invested heavily in significant awareness-raising programs in a number of these countries. As discussed below, the combination of these efforts has raised awareness to high levels throughout the region.

Examples of Output Data from Awareness Campaigns

In Belarus, the Mass Information Campaign conducted by the IOM as part of USAID's Prevention of Trafficking in Persons in Belarus, included the design and placement of 160,000 leaflets, 10,000 posters, and 35 billboards, as well as the production or sponsorship of 340 lectures, four television programs (focusing on labor migration and stigma towards VoTs), public service announcements, and a visual arts contest.

In the Central Asia region, the lead implementer of the Combating Trafficking in Persons project, IOM, reported that in Kazakhstan during one quarterly reporting period alone, the project's local NGO partners held 89 training sessions and information dissemination and awareness-raising events that were attended by 3,563 participants. The NGOs published 10 articles and 29 advertisements in newspapers and appeared on nine television programs.

Similarly, NGOs operating hotlines have amassed substantial call statistics. The NGO-operated hotlines in Kazakhstan, for example, received 3,766 calls from April to June, 2005. IOM's Counter-Trafficking Project in

Ukraine assisted 28,000 hotline callers with safe migration information or referrals from 2004 to 2006. In Belarus, the La Strada hotline, which has been in operation since 2001, has received over 12,000 phone calls.

This small sample reflects a much larger collection of data measuring output gathered by USAID projects in the region. It merely begins to suggest the sweep and penetration of awareness-related activities in E&E countries. While the scale of use of awareness campaigns is striking, it is difficult to assess the extent to which these programs have actually prevented trafficking. For example, in Kazakhstan, 19 hotlines operated by NGO partners of IOM between December 2001 and September 2003 received 25,000 calls, most of which were calls from potential migrants. Only two percent of the calls referred explicitly to "trafficking" (Kelly, 2003:91-2). This does not necessarily mean that there is no anti-trafficking benefit to the 98 percent of calls that did not refer explicitly to trafficking. However, the demonstrable output success of awareness-raising projects leads to the question, discussed later in this chapter, of what can be inferred from output measures vis-à-vis prevention objectives.

In addition to broad outreach and awareness raising for the general population, information and awareness about TIP is also imparted through structured training and educational programs. Three important avenues for such projects are training for journalists; awareness-raising sessions for public officials, local community, and religious leaders; and educational programs for children in schools.[9]

By all accounts, efforts to raise awareness have been very successful throughout the E&E region. In Albania, an assessment of USAID's CAAHT program found that 100 percent of research respondents indicated awareness of at least one anti-trafficking message, and 84 percent of respondents reported that a specific message was addressed to them (Somach & Surtees, 2005).

A similarly high percentage of study participants in the Russian Federation were found to have been reached by trafficking informational messages: "Over 80 percent of respondents in the Russian Federation have heard of potential risks associated with exploitation and trafficking of those migrating" (Tyuryukanova, 2006).[10]

A 2006 IOM report that focused on levels of awareness in Belarus, Bulgaria, Moldova, Romania, and Ukraine, confirmed "high levels" of awareness of human trafficking in the five countries. It found "general awareness of human trafficking" to be at the following levels: 88 percent in Moldova, 78 percent in Ukraine,[11] 83 percent in Belarus,[12] 83 percent in Romania, and 87 percent in Bulgaria.

Employment and Income-Producing Strategies

Local and national unemployment, severe underemployment, or unsustainable economic circumstances are commonly identified in human trafficking discourse as the catalysts for seeking better financial opportunities outside of an individual's current location. While the presence of these factors is, generally speaking, well documented, studies have noted that the notion that human trafficking is caused by "low income" or "poverty" is simplistic. A more nuanced understanding of the interplay between objective and subjective economic considerations must be established in order to create effective prevention and assistance programs.[13] Profiles of assisted victims show, for example, that many trafficking victims held jobs just before or when they were trafficked (Surtees, 2005; Surtees, 2008b). At the same time, it has been observed that the very poor probably do not make attractive targets for traffickers, as they may not be healthy or strong enough to generate substantial profits for traffickers (Bales, 2005:10). These profiles clearly suggest that other factors come into consideration, both related and unrelated to employment and financial circumstances, when individuals make the decisions that ultimately lead to being trafficked (see e.g., Lazaroiu and Alexandru, 2003).

Vocational programs that assist in job placement are the centerpiece of a number of large prevention programs in the E&E region. The services provided may include workshops on job search strategies and assistance with resume writing and interviewing techniques, training seminars on job skills development and entrepreneurship, vocational and technical skills courses, internships and mentoring programs, job placement assistance, and post-employment counseling. Typically, these programs also have empowerment components that address self-esteem and self-confidence as issues for "potential victims."

The aim of such vocational programs is to provide individuals with a means of economic self-sufficiency. They are also intended to reduce or negate some economic concerns and to provide participants with the tools they need to better protect themselves in their personal and professional lives from disempowering, risky, or dangerous circumstances.

For example, in Moldova, USAID funds Winrock International's New Perspectives for Women, a multiyear project that "aims to reduce the criminal trade in human beings by addressing the economic roots of trafficking and improving the access of young women and girls aged 16 to 25 to employment opportunities within Moldova" (www.winrock.org/md).

Utilizing Regional Support Centers (RSCs) within Moldova, the program "provides walk-in consultations, training in trafficking prevention, skills courses, short and long term employment and entrepreneurship training, internship programs and assists in the development of peer support groups" (Winrock International & UNDP, 2007).

Components of this economic empowerment program include:

- Individual consultations for women on issues related to employment and entrepreneurship such as resume writing, job search strategies, interviewing and drafting business plans;
- One- and two-day Leadership for Employment and Leadership for Entrepreneurship training seminars;
- Skills courses in areas such as computer literacy, accounting, and tailoring; and
- Mentoring and internship programs.

Through May 2006, reported examples of the program's outputs connected to economic self-sufficiency included more than 3,300 women who had received training in employability and entrepreneurship and more than 2,900 women who had received business, psychological, and legal consultations.

Of course, the ultimate objective is to find sustainable income-generating opportunities, and the program's data suggest initial signs of success on this point. Winrock reported that "329 young women and girls found employment, and more than a hundred established [their] own business."[14]

In Russia, the USAID-funded "Path to Success" program also offered courses "under the guidance of the local NGOs with careful consideration of the candidate's inclinations and the local employment situation. . . Most commonly chosen courses are those related [to] computer literacy, accountancy, sales, and hairdressing" (IOM, 2008).

The prevention value of these employment assistance and training projects is based on achieving results that lower the incidence of trafficking by helping potential VoTs to find local employment and become financially secure. This line of reasoning, however, is based upon a number of critical assumptions that, if unmet, can undermine the success of these efforts. These assumptions include:

1. Local job availability (i.e., in the area where the individual lives and the training occurs)

2. Suitable and sufficient training to help participants obtain available local jobs
3. Desirability of graduates of training programs as employees to local employers
4. Desirability of available jobs to program graduates
5. Jobs that provide graduates with a sustainable financial livelihood
6. Local jobs that are preferable to jobs abroad and that alleviate the desire or need to migrate

In contrast to achieving other worthwhile objectives such as increased knowledge of business practices or raised confidence and self-esteem, to be effective at preventing trafficking, projects need to recognize and ensure that these conditions are satisfied. Each of these assumptions must be met to bolster the success of these efforts.

Even when success is clear, however, an assessment of the far-reaching Path to Success program in Russia encapsulates the difficulty of ascertaining the impact of these programs:

> *Since the number of job placements and increased earnings were not systematically tracked, only anecdotal results are known. Most of the focus group participants from job readiness and professional trainings had found employment, although mostly on their own initiative. Information on job placements and increased earnings was not systematically recorded, so the impact of the job readiness trainings is largely anecdotal.* (Somach, 2007:8-10)

Clearly, USAID has made a major commitment to employment-based projects in the E&E region as a method to prevent TIP and these projects have shown successes in initial placement of graduates.

Income Generation and Entrepreneurial Programs

The entrepreneurial components of employment assistance programs face the challenge that although they are positive in general and achieve specific project objectives (e.g., trainings conducted, business plans written), demonstrating that TIP has been prevented by these programs is problematic. Program documents have reported mostly short-term or anecdotal examples of successes. It is important for entrepreneurial and income-generating approaches to begin to show longer-term prevention-related impact.

In Russia, Somach notes that because income generation and entrepreneurial courses have a "relatively long duration (from 3 weeks to 3 months) and higher cost, entrepreneurship training was offered to a rather small number of women. And, most of those trained did not actually start businesses (only 15% in Krasnodar)" (Somach, 2007:13). Program indicators for this component measured such aspects as: 1) number of women trained in basic job skills; 2) number of women trained in small enterprise development; and 3) number of small grants awarded to the start-up of new businesses. Somach concludes that "none of these indicators . . . measured the change in human lives and it is difficult to say if the participants became less vulnerable to becoming victims of trafficking" (Somach, 2007:14).

If business success does not happen or is transitory, an unintended consequence of heightened risk of TIP may follow. For example, if a business start-up fails and goes into debt, the individual might consider migrating in order to pay off that debt. If the individual's business skills are sharpened and the individual finds that these skills are more marketable abroad, the individual may choose to migrate to earn money and thereby place him/herself at risk of being trafficked.

Accordingly, there appear to be many potentially positive effects of these programs for the individuals participating in them, and therefore good reasons exist to continue to support their work. Nevertheless, despite the general positive impact, the level of overall trafficking risk reduction and concrete prevention results generated by these programs is not established by any data.

Empowerment Programs and Improved Community Life

Empowerment programs target young people in order to improve their community lives, social skills, and interpersonal relations. Building confidence and self-esteem is often an important element of these programs. The TIP prevention components of such programs may combine awareness training, which is intended to help participants make informed decisions in order to reduce the risk of human trafficking, with a focus on addressing deficiencies in personal and social skills that may heighten vulnerability to trafficking. These programs also provide activities that serve as temporary safe environments from potential traffickers.

Empowerment programs address a range of issues that negatively impact the lives of children and youth such as leaving school, family problems, abuse and violence, stigma, and exclusion, among others. Examples of the types of approaches utilized include counseling, educational projects, after-school programs, and summer camps.

An example of summer camps for Roma children in Albania illustrates the implementation of these various activities:

> *[V]ulnerable children in Albania spend a lot of time working and begging on the street, which limits their educational and recreational opportunities and negatively impacts on their intellectual and physical development. Life on the street is either a form of trafficking or exposes children to the risk of trafficking or other forms of exploitation. Summer camps serve as a mechanism to prevent children from going to work on the street in the summer months and instead affords them educational and recreational opportunities in their communities. The programmes have been implemented jointly by Roma and non-Roma NGOs.* (Surtees, 2006b)

Empowerment and community improvement programs provide young people with the ability to make better choices in the job market, which may prevent them from pursuing unrealistic offers of riches abroad (Rosenberg, 2004:18). Empowerment programs are not unique to anti-trafficking projects. Many agencies and organizations, such as the United Nations, support empowerment programs that, organized as "camps" that focuse on sports or the arts, promote positive inter-ethnic relations for youth.[15]

The prevention benefits of empowerment programs are indirect, and these programs probably would be implemented in a number of countries whether or not they were associated with preventing trafficking in persons. One question that arises is in what circumstances and to what extent should funding that is dedicated to the prevention of human trafficking be relied upon as the exclusive funding support of clearly cross-cutting activities such as summer camps. Perhaps anti-TIP funds should be used to develop TIP prevention modules and activities that could be adapted for and incorporated into concurrent programs that focus on empowerment or improved community life.

In her 2004 report, Rosenberg observed that while positive impressions about the impact of these projects were common, no one could document prevention impact. Certainly more can and should be done to obtain evidence of positive outcomes. At a minimum, follow-ups should be conducted with participating children six months and one year after participation, to the extent possible and appropriate. However, it is likely that unless donors are willing to support a long-term study by experienced researchers that examines the longer-term trajectory of the lives of children participating in these programs (even at points in time after the specific implementing projects may have ended), data revealing long-term outcomes among participants will not likely be available for analysis. Thus, the impact of such programs will be unknowable, and the role and value of empowerment programs as a prevention method against TIP will remain uncertain.

Crisis Prevention and Family Violence Mitigation Programs

Family violence and other crisis intervention programs are intended to provide critical support that can reduce family conflict and violence while addressing other personal crises that may prevent individual family members from making decisions and taking actions that could heighten the risk of or lead to being trafficked. Crisis interventions are an important component of several USAID-sponsored projects in the E&E region.

In Albania and Greece, the TACT project works comprehensively with children and families at risk.[16] TdH recognizes that the family, not just the individual, holds part of the key to successful prevention of trafficking, especially regarding child trafficking. TdH has trained crisis prevention workers to pay regular visits to families who are the project's beneficiaries. Through social counseling, these family visits have raised awareness among parents about their children's rights and led to discussions of child trafficking and the consequences of child exploitation. These family visits allow workers to maintain regular contact with families, convince parents to enroll their children in school, and keep track of the further developments within the families. In total, there have been 15,400 family visits paid in Albania and Greece, out of which 620 were conducted together with the municipal social services (TdH, 2006). TdH's work with families extends beyond these visits to include help with food for the family and material assistance to encourage children to go to school or to vocational training.

In Ukraine, the multi-year USAID-sponsored Crisis Prevention Program (CPP), which was implemented by Winrock, described the strategy of crisis prevention and violence mitigation projects this way:

> *In an effort to assist potential trafficking victims as well as women who have returned from working abroad, this project focused on other factors that might increase the likelihood of a woman accepting a job offer abroad. For example, women may look to employment opportunities abroad as a means of escape from a crisis situation. Women returning from working abroad often*

need assistance dealing with traumas resulting from their experiences abroad. (Winrock, 2004:10)

The CPP provided a variety of services to women in crisis situations, including trainings on trafficking prevention and violence prevention, which incorporate elements of women's leadership and human rights training to empower women; walk-in, personalized services including free information on trafficking in women, referral services to physicians and psychologists, pro bono legal consultations, and support groups for women experiencing similar situations; and free telephone information hotlines operated by the Centers (Winrock, 2004:10). The CPP reported the following activities and outputs:

- Total participating in nation-wide trafficking and violence prevention training seminars – 30,148;
- Total hotline calls received – 70,208, of which nine percent of callers had concerns about violence and 12 percent of callers were calling about relationship issues;
- During one reporting quarter, a total of 112 people participated in self-help groups at the seven Crisis Intervention Centers. The self-help groups provided women with the support they needed to be able to speak out, make informed decisions, and become more self-confident;
- From 2004 to mid-2008, a total of 29,876 women took advantage of the walk-in services provided at the Centers. During the reporting quarter, a total of 2,209 women used the CPP walk-in services for the first time. The majority of consultations were provided to victims of human trafficking and their relatives.

Again, despite the importance of these activities (and those of other similar projects in the E&E region), data have not been systematically gathered and analyzed by project implementers (or independent researchers) to assess the long-term trafficking prevention impact based upon behavioral or other changes due to these interventions.

Safe Migration Programs – Educating, Advising and Job Vetting

Programs aimed at promoting safe, legal migration are often touted as key to anti-trafficking prevention because many cases of trafficking involve criminals intercepting individuals intent on migrating and manipulating the migration process to serve their human trafficking objectives.

Safe migration programs are designed to address the problem of trafficking through seminars, distribution of "safe migration" awareness documents, and answering questions in response to helpline calls or at clinics. Common techniques that individuals are encouraged to utilize to protect themselves from deceitful job offers that veil trafficking schemes include:

1. Verify whether a job agency or opportunity is legitimate;
2. Ask for an employment contract;
3. Have someone – preferably a lawyer – review a contract and comment on it;
4. Review and sign a contract for employment;
5. Leave a copy of the contract with relatives or friends;
6. Leave a copy of a passport with relatives or friends;
7. Leave contact information with relatives or friends;
8. Leave the employer's contact information with relatives or friends;
9. Create a password/code language to let people know: "I'm in trouble";
10. Attend a career counseling session. (Boak et al., 2003:95)

Safe migration projects are necessary; a growing number of studies find that most individuals will migrate regardless of programs sensitizing them to the risk of human trafficking. The critical question, then, is to what degree can specific "tips" promote an informed and vigilant migration experience that protects migrants against human trafficking.

The desired outcome of safe migration programs is that a migrating individual's behavior is consistent with protecting himself or herself. It is hoped that migrating individuals are enabled to recognize and make a series of decisions that will avert their being trafficked. The following paragraph illustrates the type of results these programs seek to achieve:

> *[C]lients of the NGO West Ukrainian Center "Women's Perspectives" in Ukraine had provided advice to two girls who had been offered jobs as dancers in Japan through a Polish company. As a result of this advice, the girls requested and received roundtrip tickets and refused to relinquish their passports on arrival. Soon after arriving, they met other girls from Ukraine and Russia whom they believed had been forced into prostitution. The girls ran away and used their tickets to return to Ukraine. The company contacted them and asked them to return the money for the travel, but the lawyer from*

the center wrote a letter outlining the numerous contract violations that had taken place and refusing to give back the money. The company has not contacted the girls again. (Rosenberg, 2004:21)

In this anecdote, the young women took several "safe migration" actions such as refusing to relenquish their passports and arranging roundtrip tickets that preserved their ability to take action on their own behalves to protect themselves.[17]

In the past few years, little progress in establishing the impact of "safe migration" strategies has been made. Whether projects engaged in safe migration or job-vetting services have undertaken (or been expected to undertake) any gathering of data beyond isolated anecdotal stories of success is not apparent. Such stories are helpful for illustrative purposes but are not the same as documented results. Significantly, no data appear to exist, for example, regarding to what extent VoTs received migration information prior to being trafficked. This lack of information prevents USAID and others from assessing the impact of safe migration or job-vetting services on TIP prevention or to determine approaches that might be viewed as best practices in terms of preventing TIP.

A substantial number of anti-TIP, migration, and labor programs are sponsored by various governments in countries of origin and destination. Within that combined effort, it should be possible to improve the collection and analysis of data about the factors and circumstances, apart from the criminal intervention of a trafficker, that differentiate an individual who migrates successfully, for example, from one who is trafficked,.

Recognizing the limits of various steps in TIP prevention in order to avoid a false sense of security on the part of a potential VoTs is important. For example, while an inability to secure an employment contract prior to travel is one signal that something suspicious may be afoot, the opposite is not necessarily true. A signed employment contract does not protect against being trafficked; and a trafficker who, by definition, will resort to deception or coercion to achieve his or her criminal objective would not hesitate to provide a document purporting to be an employment contract to the targeted individual.

Additionally, confiscating a passport is a prevalent means of exerting control over a VoT. Safe migration programs counsel individuals not to give up their passports. While awareness of the potential danger of not keeping control of one's passport is important, it is also necessary to consider how many points during travel or migration at which relenquishing one's passport temporarily is expected and even necessary. Travelers are asked for their passports in all sorts of apparently inoccuous contexts – when checking into a hotel, for example. Whether or not to relenquish the passport becomes a question of the danger of promoting a false sense of security. In the context of well-orchestrated deceptions, possible corruption (e.g., border and immigration officials or travel service or hotel employees), and/or forced passport confiscation by criminals, counseling individuals on the wisdom of holding onto one's passport seems inadequate to the task of meaningful TIP prevention in real-world settings. Are individuals also counseled on how to respond to what may appear to be regular and accepted requests to provide the passport, but which may (or may not) be part of a trafficking scheme? When, in those circumstances, should suspicion arise? What should the individual do at that point? Safe migration advice is important, but it is also critical to review more thoroughly the sufficiency and applicability of such advice in the context of the realities of how VoTs are trafficked.

In addition to the range of steps that individuals are encouraged to take to avoid TIP, a second component of an ideal safe migration strategy involves job vetting by a trustworthy NGO to confirm the existence and safety of a job offer. It appears that job vetting is a promising, albeit underutilized, method of prevention assistance to individuals in countries of origin. Since job vetting requires inquiry into employment in various countries of destination, this is a labor-intensive, time-consuming, and potentially costly approach to prevention. Nevertheless, it is worth examining whether cooperative partnerships between NGOs in countries of origin and those in countries of destination can develop in order to vet jobs in destination countries. Consideration could also be given to whether job vetting is a prevention approach for which government-NGO partnerships could be developed.

Demand Reduction

Prevention focusing on demand seeks to reduce TIP by addressing demand for commercial sex as well as exploitable labor in sectors such as agriculture and construction. These methods seek to change attitudes and behavior by those who create the demand: e.g., customers, employers, end-users, purchasers, and clients.

Comprehensive TIP prevention strategies should include a component that addresses demand.[18] A succinct statement of the strategic rationale for countering demand-side factors is found in "U.S. Government Efforts to Fight Demand Fueling Human Trafficking":

> *While no precise definiton of demand for human trafficking exists, for the purposes of this fact sheet, demand can take two forms: 1) that of the trafficker or "wholesaler" whose greed motivates the victimization of vulnerable individuals; and 2) that of the consumer whose demand determines profitablilty. Market demand for commercial sex acts and cheap labor create a profit-incentive for traffickers to entrap more victims, fueling the growth of trafficking in persons.* (U.S. Department of State, 2008)

To date, demand-based strategies have targeted men in the general population. As well, a number of intergovernmental organizations – the UN, OSCE, and NATO – for example, have enacted standards to regulate the actions of military and peacekeeping personnel. Related efforts focusing on peacekeeping forces have been undertaken in Bosnia and Kosovo. In particular, training and awareness campaigns have been initiated (see e.g., United Nations, 2004).

One multi-country project focusing on promoting legislative reform and related activities to address demand for prostitution was identified. No E&E project specifically addressing demand for labor trafficking directly was identified.

The U.S. Department of State (G/TIP) is funding an awareness and advocacy project implemented by the European Women's Lobby and the Coalition against Trafficking in Women (CATW) that seeks to prevent sex trafficking by reducing demand for prostitution. The project utilizes a variety of measures, including awareness campaigns and advocating for changes in laws to criminalize the buyer and decriminalize the seller of sex.[19]

While no authoritative data on the effectiveness of demand reduction strategies in countries of the E&E region yet exist, a study of men in Kosovo who had used the services of a prostitute within the preceding 12 months found that most were aware of the trafficking problem (Prism, 2007: 67). Thus, their awareness of trafficking (or that the women might have been trafficked) did not necessarily translate into behavioral changes vis-à-vis prostitution. On the other hand, one report observed fewer trafficking cases in Bosnia and Herzegovina and attributed this to reduced demand:

> *The peacekeepers who are still based in BiH enjoy much less freedom of movement and are not able to visit bars and other places known for prostitution. Very few cases have been identified of women being trafficked*

> *from the Eastern European countries (Moldova, Romania, Bulgaria and Ukraine) which accounted for most of the victims in the past. There are also almost no cases of new arrivals from those countries: the women who were identified recently arrived in BiH many years ago (at least five years ago) and stayed in different bars in BiH or in other countries of the region, all this time working in prostitution.* (GAATW, 2007:69)

While demand-based prevention methods are important as part of a comprehensive strategy, in order to recognize which methods are effective it is important to untangle the mix of variables that can be at play.[20] In this case, for example, demand reduction strategies aimed at military and peace keeping forces may be different from those aimed at the general population (i.e., the amount of "free" time of the men is limited, specific locations can be placed on off-limits lists and under the watchful eye of military police).

In short, there are no in-depth objective studies in the region that can inform future programming aimed at reducing demand by helping to determine what works, what does not, and why. Going forward, conducting such a review of the effectiveness of particular demand approaches will be valuable.

Protection as Prevention

The return of a trafficked individual to his or her country of origin potentially places him or her at risk of being re-trafficked. VoTs often return to an environment that has remained unchanged, if not worsened. The experience of being trafficked will often exacerbate issues that existed previously, including some that may have contributed to being trafficked in the first place. Additionally, returning VoTs commonly face new issues of stigma and discrimination in their home communities and even by their families.

Recent research documents the challenges of VoTs who have returned home to find that life remains difficult and the earlier risks continue:

> *I had many episodes when I wanted to drop everything and go back to the streets where I would try to make money for myself. I just had moments like this when I felt that that life was too easy. This thing on the street was in my blood. I was so used to it. . . . . When I was at home with my parents, we did not have enough to eat and I used to look out on the street and think at the choices that I had. And the street looked like a way to make money.* (Surtees, 2007)

Providing a safety net of support for returning victims acts as a means of preventing re-trafficking. IOM in Ukraine and the TACT program in Albania provide services to returning trafficked children, potential victims, and their families, with the objective of preventing both trafficking and re-trafficking. In Moldova, the USAID project assists vulnerable youth from orphanages and boarding schools by providing life-skills, job and employment training, as well as health services, counseling, and tangible work experiences (Winrock, 2007).

Projects should endeavor to measure the long-term incidence of possible re-trafficking among their beneficiaries. If appropriate and properly done, VoTs who had been beneficiaries of any service programs (related to trafficking or not) should be asked for their perspective on the relationship between their receiving those services and their being trafficked.[21] It is extremely difficult to gauge the prevention impact of the provision of services to VoTs without gathering this new data. Most important, however, the difficulties of documenting the prevention characteristics of protection programs should in no way reduce the ample need and justification for the provision of these services.

Criminal Enforcement as Prevention

Although USAID has funded some law enforcement-related projects, they are the exception more than the rule. Other parts of the United States Government such as the Department of State's Bureau of International Narcotics and Law Enforcement Affairs (INL) and the Department of Justice's Office of Overseas Prosecutorial Development, Assistance, and Training (OPDAT) support or implement various programs in the region.

Arguably, deterrence, or the crippling of criminal networks through conviction, confiscation of assets, and crime prevention techniques could be a valuable prevention component. Prosecutions are up in a number of countries in the region. However, there is no evidence that these activities have reached a threshold level that would produce a deterrence effect.

Analysis & Conclusions

The project reports and other related material reviewed for this chapter demonstrate that prevention projects in the region are touching many lives in positive ways. Nevertheless, despite the worthiness of such work, not all desirable outcomes (e.g., increased awareness, stronger job application skills, and enhanced self-esteem and empowerment) yield – or are yet being shown to yield – tangible results in terms of prevention of TIP.

The key challenge for improving prevention efforts is two-fold: 1) insufficient data and analysis on the root causes, contributing factors, vulnerabilities, and risks that may lead to trafficking in persons in its diverse manifestations for different profiles of potential victims; and 2) insufficient data and analysis on the link between prevention of trafficking in concrete ways and USAID's TIP prevention programming. By addressing these shortcomings, the effectiveness of prevention initiatives can improve; by not attending to these concerns, the effectiveness of prevention efforts will be slowed dramatically.

The remainder of this chapter discusses these challenges and identifies a number of recommendations for good practices that USAID and its implementing partners should consider, to the extent that they are not already, as possible avenues to improve the design and implementation of future prevention projects.

Understanding the Complexity of Underlying Factors

As indicated in earlier sections of this chapter, prevention work is justified, and needed, because it addresses one or more of the factors that contribute to TIP. Prevention interventions are intended to address these underlying factors or how an individual experiences and reacts to these factors in ways that pre-empt and reduce the incidence of TIP.

This mission is at least as difficult as implementing an effective criminal justice or victim assistance response. The context of risk and vulnerability in which TIP flourishes – and that prevention work seeks to alter – is extremely complicated. The breadth, pervasiveness, and in many cases intransigience of factors contributing to the existence of TIP present a serious test for all prevention activities.

The design and implementation of TIP prevention initiatives rarely account for this complexity. Instead, a relatively short list of core "root causes"[22] such as "poverty," "lack of awareness," "low education," and "demand" are routinely emphasized. The concern for those designing and implementing prevention efforts is that any "short list" of potential factors also constitutes a severely truncated list, one that risks oversimplifying the span and intracacies of factors potentially at work.[23] The degree of potential oversimplification is highlighted by stitching together a more expanded list of factors that have, at one time or another, been pointed to as causing or contributing to TIP:

- Globalization (especially the opening of previously closed borders, increasing ease of transborder transportation);
- Lack of political will to address TIP;
- Conflict and civil instability, strife, or transition;
- Displacement and dislocation (man-made and natural);
- Immigration policy (both restrictive and open migration policies);
- Family violence, both physical and psychological;
- Family instability or disintegration;
- Poverty, financial distress, lack of economic opportunity;
- Economic disparity vis-à-vis countries to which migration is possible;
- Belonging to a group marginalized by ethnicity or gender, or a lack of citizenship eligibility or birth registration;
- Lack of social safety net;
- Lack of information needed to protect oneself against TIP;
- Growth of women as sole supporters of families;
- Patriarchal attitudes and institutions;
- Demand for cheap and exploitable laborers in service, agriculture, construction, and other business and industry sectors;
- Corruption;
- High profits for traffickers (greed of criminals);
- Low risk of prosecution or conviction of traffickers; and
- Weak rule of law and government institutions.

This list is itself illustrative and partial, but it serves to suggest the sweep of factors that a comprehensive and integrated prevention strategy must consider and potentially confront for each country (and across regions).

Particularly daunting for the prospects of prevention success is that no single factor "causes" TIP.[24] TIP is the product of a multiplicity of factors that combine in different ways that are specific to the context of each country, community, family, and individual (Surtees, 2005:13; Dottridge, 2007:1; La Strada International, 2008:44).

The many social, political, and cultural factors implicated produce a number of other societal ills – not only TIP – and are often found intertwined with others. Poverty can be related to low levels of educational attainment, discrimination, obstacles to accessing credit, exploitation, and violence. Societies that have faced recent conflict often have weakened institutions and rule of law as well as pervasive corruption. Issues involving demand and globalization are intertwined (for both sex trafficking and labor trafficking). Contemplating these entanglements of factors serves as a reminder that TIP prevention does not occur in a vacuum. Ultimately, it entails consideration of how to address societal factors that contribute to or facilitate TIP but are themselves "bigger" than TIP. The intersection of factors also means that there can be no single path to prevention, and an overall prevention strategy that addresses an entangled mix of factors in a comprehensive and coherent way must be constructed.

On the other hand, the role of the individual at important junctures – for example, when making a decision to migrate or to trust an untrustworthy acquiantance or relative – along an arc of behaviors and decisions that potentially lead to TIP is not well understood, either. The subjective nature of individual decision making adds another layer of complexity to understanding what leads to cases of TIP.[25] But questions concerning what factors are included in an individual's decision, how they are perceived and weighed, and when decisions are made by an individual are all relevent to prevention efforts.[26]

Finally, more needs to be known about what factors work to counter vulnerabilities and risk to TIP. Not all "at-risk" individuals are trafficked. Not all people in similar economic circumstances, for instance, decide to migrate, thereby potentially putting themselves on an intersecting path with traffickers. Some individuals who are aware of trafficking are eventually trafficked and some are not. A portion of those who suffer past violence (of any kind) are trafficked but many are not. The majority of individuals, including children, caught in conflict situations or the aftermath of devastating natural disasters, despite the possibility of heightened risk, avoid being trafficked. Examining more systematically why some individuals from a community or group are eventually trafficked while others in prima facie indistinguishable circumstances are not may uncover promising new avenues to counter balance risks and vulnerabilities.[27]

In short, knowledge about the factors that contribute to (and counter) TIP is incomplete and, from the standpoint of the practical needs of developing prevention policy and projects, inadequate. Even as more is learned, untangling intertwined factors to assess how they may contribute to TIP (individually and in combination) will present a steep challenge for designing and implementing effective prevention efforts.

Pervasive Assumptions about Root Causes

The previous subsection describes the complex nature of root causes, contributing factors, vulnerabilities, and risks that are linked to TIP and the knowledge gap that exists about those factors.

Because so little empirical work has been done regarding these factors, many assumptions have emerged to fill the void. Common assumptions about the factors that lead to trafficking contain elements of fact, but they do not account for the full picture of what is necessary to construct more effective prevention plans against TIP.

For example, the assertion that domestic violence is a cause of human trafficking is oft-repeated by project implementers and others in the region and elsewhere. They see a pattern of past family dysfunction for a number of beneficiaries who receive assistance. It seems logical on its face that such a connection would exist. However, the most comprehensive review of assisted victims in Southeastern Europe to date found that more victims of trafficking do not report experiencing family violence and/or a positive family life (Surtees, 2005; Warnath, 2007).[28] This does not mean that no connection between TIP and serious family dysfunction, abuse, or violence exists. Rather, it suggests that we do not yet understand or account fully for the variations and subtleties of family dynamics in our discussions and approaches to TIP prevention.

Other customary working assumptions are prevalent. While many trafficking victims have "low" educational levels, this often turns out to be a level of education similar to others in their home country who were not trafficked (Surtees, 2005).[29] While many VoTs come from economically deprived backgrounds, there are cases of VoTs from families that are economically "well-off" or "average" for their communities (Surtees, 2005). And while lack of information elevates the risk of being trafficked, the large number of individuals who are trafficked multiple times is evidence of the limits of raising awareness in preventing trafficking.

In the absence of sound empirical grounding, working assumptions have been necessary. They have served a purpose by providing the possibility of roughly approximating where to locate prevention activities, at least in the initiation phases of those efforts. However, in general, prevention objectives are not best-served over the long term by largely unexamined or superficial attributions of causes to human trafficking. The danger of allowing unsound or untested assumptions to guide policy and programming decisions is that these assumptions can undermine the likelihood of obtaining meaningful results, compromise the impact of donor investments and ultimately discredit anti-trafficking policies and programs.

Better Evidence about Factors Contributing to Trafficking in Persons

The foregoing discussion reveals a need to more systematically and rigorously examine the role of factors that underlie TIP to support the ability to reduce and ultimately eradicate trafficking. To close the gap in knowledge about factors that facilitate or lead to trafficking, better data and analysis is required.

a. There Is a Need for More and Better Data to Determine How Factors Contribute to Trafficking in Persons

Substantial information about TIP already has been collected in the E&E region. Notwithstanding this, the suitability of current data needed to uncover the elements leading to TIP appear limited.

One reason for this limited data is that the informaton is collected predominately from VoTs by NGO service providers during the assistance process. Service providers, however, rarely gather data in the detail necessary to illuminate issues of cause and effect. This is understandable given that the primary mission for most of these organizations is providing care for victims, not conducting in-depth research. Moreover, as a practical matter, few local service providers have the capacity or support of donors to add the more labor intensive detailed inquiries required to serve the objectives of research over and above the data gathered to support their responsibilities of providing care.

Consider several examples based upon common inquiries from case management intake questionnaires: little, if any, information relevent to prevention planning can be discerned by learning that TIP recruitment was arranged by an individual who was classified, based upon undefined or undisclosed criteria, as an "acquaintance." Prevention planning would seek greater detail and disaggregation of the category of acquaintance. Similarly, service providers typically do not ask beneficiaries for specifics about family relations and dynamics beyond seeking a yes/no response to the question of whether the individual had experienced family violence anytime prior to being trafficked. But a yes/no answer, without more information, cannot establish family violence as a "cause" of trafficking. Other data relevant to the question of establishing a causal link, such as the timeframe of that violence in relation to the act of being trafficked, are needed and generally have not been collected.

The data relied upon to infer root causes also may be based upon interview questions posed that reflect prevailing assumptions, thus rendering the data less suitable for testing those same assumptions. Consider, for instance, how the assumptions identified in the previous section may unintentionally be built into interview questionnaires. A questionnaire to construct an individual's case management file may confirm a low education or income level, but it would not place that data in the comparative context of the communities from which the individual originated. Similarly, a questionnaire for case management purposes would be most interested in a history of a dysfunctional or abusive family relationship. But this would miss potential information that could reveal to what extent the opposite may be true: i.e., that strong and supportive family relations can contribute to trafficking by empowering an individual, as a result of that family support, to relish the prospect of embarking out in the world. Or that strong family ties may compel individuals to leave their home communities to support their families by seeking financial opportunities elsewhere.

There are reasons to be cautious about the suitability of current data to determine what leads to incidences of TIP. Most research is based upon the data pool of VoTs who have been identified and receive assistance. Risks arise, however, in assuming too much about what can be known about vulnerability from the data collected only from assisted VoTs. This data pool does not include the larger body of undiscovered VoTs or the many identified VoTs who do not agree to accept assistance. Thus, the data pool of almost all current research is made up of a select subgroup of all victims, which may or may not represent the entire category of VoTs.

Consider how the simple fact of utilizing a data pool of only assisted VoTs may skew our understanding of the causes of trafficking and our sense of what is required for prevention. Research shows that one major reason that some identified VoTs do not accept assistance is that they have good family relations. They either have a family support net that they can return to or, alternatively, they refuse shelter-based assistance because they have family members to support (Brunovskis & Surtees, 2007). Thus, the experience of these VoTs may diverge from the family portrait of many in the pool of VoTs who accepted assistance. This can distort the comparative percentages of VoTs classified as from "healthy" or "good" families versus dysfunctional or abusive families.

Finally, knowledge of VoTs' backgrounds, and therefore contributing factors to VoTs' trafficking, is largely limited to the beneficiary population primarily served by shelter assistance programs: single young women who have been victims of sex trafficking. The restricted scope of beneficiary groups served leaves gaps in the knowledge base about potential victims who do not conform to the more standardized profile (for example, men, minors/children of different ages, married women, women with children, those who are trafficking into forced labor, begging and other non-sex trafficking scenarios). These gaps represent a large segment of the overall problem of TIP in the region and globally and are underserved by prevention activities.

b. There Is a Need for Better Analysis of How Different Factors Contribute to Trafficking in Persons

Understanding the factors contributing to TIP in ways that will improve prevention requires more than collecting better data. It also requires the application of more sophisticated analysis to that data. TIP studies need to move beyond attributing causal weight to any factor that is simply found to precede instances of TIP; they must help to explain the relative roles and/or interactions of the many preceding factors in ways that can help focus anti-TIP prevention efforts to become more effective.

When more penetrating research and analysis is conducted, interesting insights emerge that suggest the potential of research to help policymakers, donors, and practitioners in practical ways. For example, a study in Romania reviewed how dropping out of school could be a point of vulnerability for young women or girls. Among other things, it found that dropping out of school emerges as a vulnerability factor in different ways for girls living on their own than for girls living with their families. For those living with their families, vulnerability arose more from the desire for independence and self-sufficiency. In contrast, for young women living on their own, material considerations were more central in fueling frustrations that created vulnerability (Centre for Urban and Regional Research et al., excerpt undated). Eliciting these types of more subtle differentiations through better research and analysis leads to the possibility of more tailored and targeted prevention efforts.

Similarly, a USAID assessment in Russia (Somach, 2007) identified a subgroup within the overarching category of "young women" who, it was suggested, were particularly vulnerable to being recruited in TIP schemes based upon the nature of their employment: "Young people, especially young women, working as waitresses in cafes or restaurants – recruiters have a captive audience while they are at work" (Somach, 2007:18).

Targeting At-Risk Groups More Precisely

With a better understanding of the factors that lead to TIP comes the ability to identify categories of groups "at-risk" with great precision. In turn, this permits targeting more effectively prevention activities to individuals within those groups.

a. Prevention Projects Target At-Risk Groups too Broadly

At present, many projects in the region use broad parameters to identify as "at-risk" groups to be targeted by their prevention activities.[30] This is illustrated in a recent project report narrative by a major international organization conducting a USAID prevention program. It indicates that the project was directed toward the following "target populations":

- Children;
- General population;
- Special populations;
- Non-governmental organizations/private voluntary organizations;
- Populations vulnerable to trafficking;
- Victims of trafficking; and
- Youth (aged 15 to 24).

Identifying at-risk populations with too broad a brush, as is exemplified here, is common. These types of classifications are too generic and sweeping to provide meaningful direction for effective targeting of prevention programming. It is difficult to envision who would not be included within the scope of the cumulatively "targeted" populations of such a prevention effort.

It will be necessary, as a first step toward meaningful targeting, to revisit overarching "at-risk" categories to disaggregate them in ways intended to advance prevention objectives. The process of refining target classifications should be evidence-based and specific to projects undertaken in each country (and ideally each community) in the E&E region.[31]

b. Neglected Groups Need to Be Incorporated into Prevention Strategies

In addition to aiming prevention efforts more precisely within overarching categories of "at-risk" groups, more effective targeting efforts also may expose additional categories that need the attention of prevention projects.

As discussed above, current prevention strategies focus heavily on young women and minimizing or disrupting the threat of sex trafficking. This represents only one slice, however significant, of the trafficking problem. Men, minors of various ages, members of ethnic minorities,[32] among other groups have not been fully included in the design and implementation of prevention programs across the region, nor has the range of forms of trafficking received the full attention of prevention efforts across the region. This has begun to change to some degree, but signficant gaps remain.[33]

In addition, prevention efforts currently exclude some populations based upon geography rather than assessments of comparative risks of populations. This shortfall appears, with some exceptions, in the continued inability to reach many residents in rural or minority communities with prevention efforts, such as helpline coverage, economic-based prevention projects, or dissemination of prevention material that is linguistically and culturally appropriate for the specific population in the particular geographic area. Because geographic remoteness does not diminish the risk of being trafficked, prevention efforts viewed as necessary to provide information or financial opportunities to allow individuals to better protect themselves against the dangers of trafficking in one part of a country, for example, are probably also necessary, in some form, in other uncovered parts of the country.

Expanding coverage of prevention projects to include currently underserved groups will place more demands on the projects. To help address this, it would be useful to review opportunities to expand working partnerships with existing national and/or local government and NGO projects in a more integrated and coordinated manner. More integration and coordination of efforts would permit more efficient, effective, and sustainable delivery of prevention efforts. Opportunities to reach across borders to extend useful cooperative efforts should be further examined as well. One example of this cross-border cooperation occurred in several instances when hotlines were extended with toll-free service over a wider geographic area.

Links between Activities and Outcomes are Not Established

The previous subsection discusses limits to what is known about the various risk factors that are associated with the likelihood that an individual will be trafficked. Similarly, what is known currently about the relationship between prevention program activities and prevention impact is tenuous. Despite the difficulties of showing prevention results, well-constructed research as well as monitoring and evaluation will go a long way toward providing the signposts needed to make prevention efforts more effective.

Currently little, if any, evidence is available that TIP is abating in the E&E region or around the globe. In this context, the basic, but most important, question arises: "How do we know if our efforts to prevent TIP are working?"

While this question needs to be answered for every project, this is not a question that can (or should) be answered solely within the "four walls" of individual projects. Unfortunately, the structure of individual projects, which is short-term, stand-alone, fragmented and incremental, is not conducive to gauging long-term durable prevention results.[34]

As long as activities, data gathering, analysis, and evaluation of activities are organized in the limited way that they are today, the possibility of answering the question of whether we are achieving prevention results will be inhibited. This, in turn, will hinder the prospects of learning enough about our anti-TIP efforts to better equip those efforts to match the nature of the problem and thereby better enable those efforts to serve long-term prevention objectives.

a. Research Is Needed to Strengthen the Links between Prevention Activities and Results

A number of positive changes in attitudes and behaviors of many participants in anti-TIP projects have been described by organizations implementing those projects and others, to a lesser extent. These descriptions, however promising, are nevertheless different from showing prevention results. Demonstrating the effectiveness of prevention programs is difficult and, to date, has remained problematic.

The difficulty of establishing solid links between project activities and prevention results begs the question of whether current activities directed at reducing one, two, or more of the apparent vulnerabilities or risk factors are more than blunt instruments for preventing human trafficking. Many lines of inquiry could help to clarify this connection. For example, research could begin by addressing the following topics:

- How many VoTs in the region were exposed previously to prevention activities? What do they say about their experience regarding the relationship between the prevention activity and their subsequently being trafficked?
- Do graduates of safe migration projects subsequently migrate safely and avoid being ensnared in trafficking?
- What is the level and quality of interventions for the purpose of TIP prevention by border and immigration officials trained to identify trafficking cases at points of entry? How does this compare to prevention interventions at the border by untrained officials? When a potential TIP case was detected, did the prevention efforts extend to launching a pro-active investigation to uncover the other perpetrators involved to shut down the trafficking scheme before other victims were ensnared?
- Similarly, for projects addressing demand reduction, how strong is the empirical relationship between activity directed at prostitution or economic exploitation in labor and the reduction of TIP?

Research that has taken even a cursory look at the connection between specific prevention activities and the likelihood of reducing trafficking in at-risk groups has illuminated the need to bring more rigor to the examination. For example, prevention messages are increasingly incorporated into school curricula or other activities because of the potential vulnerability of children and the apparent efficiency of using schools for education about TIP. This can be an effective prevention approach. However, research conducted in Albania in 2005 found that most trafficked children in that country had little education or had never attended school (Somach and Surtees, 2005). The research also found that although trafficked children were primarily Egyptian and Roma minorities, the children who participated in TIP awareness programs were largely ethnic Albanians.

Similarly, entrepreneurial training programs, despite demonstrable benefits in general, may only be indirectly and tenuously linked to benefiting the primary profiles of at-risk groups identified by prevention projects. Instead, research has found that they appear to benefit categories of women who are older and fall outside current primary age-groups targeted by prevention projects (Somach, 2007; Rosenberg, 2004; Callender et al., 2002-3).

b. Monitoring and Evaluation Is Necessary to Establish Links between Prevention Activity and Results

Aside from developing a body of research to elicit information about the effectiveness of prevention approaches, a critical need remains to make monitoring and evaluation ("M&E") a core component of prevention projects. In the E&E region, as in other regions around the world, most projects do not include the application of a satisfactory M&E approach.

The value of M&E in the context of TIP projects is widely recognized. M&E is an indispensable tool for aiding decision-making that aims to fundamentally improve future iterations of prevention programs. The lessons learned from solid M&E help future projects to identify and replicate the successful elements of earlier projects and improve upon areas that were identified as less effective. M&E provides critical information to support the achievement of project and policy objectives. It highlights strengths and weakness of project efforts, permits corrections, identifies effectiveness, and informs project replication and sustainability.[35] Ultimately, the benefits of good monitoring and assessments will be tangible. On the other hand, implementing prevention projects without also generating and analyzing sound M&E information about their activities renders them at risk of being haphazard.

Transitioning to widespread application of meaningful M&E presents substantial challenges. M&E needs to be incorporated as part of the project design from the beginning and in many cases, would involve evaluation activities that could extend years beyond a project's life. It can be costly and involve labor-intensive planning and implementation. At the same time, a well-thought out M&E approach should be undertaken in ways that support the efforts of project staff and do not divert them from the core mission of their projects.

The principal challenge for prevention projects, and what has been missing so far for most projects, is the development of: 1) baselines and 2) outcome indicators that are specific, meaningful, and measurable.

Despite the challenge, a pressing need remains to develop credible approaches to establishing baselines. These baselines will provide a foundation for future exercises to identify promising, good, or best practices among projects. The two go hand-in-hand. Donors and others who stress, with good reason, the imperative that projects show signs of progress resulting from the investments made need to also recognize that the capacity to measure such progress depends upon and must be preceded by tangible support for the creation of baselines against which to compare the consequences of actions taken.

Equally necessary for measuring progress is clarifying the fuzziness of the line between output measurements and measures of prevention results for many projects. Currently, measuring the "success" of prevention projects focuses nearly exclusively on describing process and counting outputs (e.g., number of posters printed, number of participants trained). Outputs are useful, especially in assessing whether activities conform to the initial project design for activities to be undertaken. Outputs are not sufficient indicators, however, of a project's value measured in terms of its impact. There is a need to supplement process and output tabulations with a bright-line focus on impact evaluations to illustrate positive and negative results, as well as intended and unintended consequences.

New Strategies are Needed to Transform Awareness into Prevention

USAID-sponsored TIP awareness projects have grown significantly in reach and breadth in countries of the E&E region since they were first initiated there approximately ten years ago. The high levels of awareness reported in a number of countries are a testament to the success of efforts to disseminate information about TIP.

At the same time, studies have demonstrated that many VoTs were aware of trafficking, because of awareness campaigns, but decided to migrate nevertheless and were subsequently trafficked. All research focused on this issue calls into question the degree to which increased awareness produces changes in decisions or behaviors that reduce TIP when other circumstances (e.g., economic need, violent environment) remain unchanged (see e.g., Brunovskis & Surtees, 2007:117-18). The research suggests that prevention impact may be marginal because knowledge of potential individual risk is either discounted or overridden by other considerations. Many VoTs believed that trafficking could not happen to them, or they decided to take the risk (out of financial desperation or for other reasons). The challenge now is making anti-trafficking messages more effective in achieving prevention. Given the migration context in a number of E&E countries, how to take this transition to a new level of effectiveness is not clear.

A first step is to consider adjusting strategies once extremely high levels of awareness have been achieved in a country. Message saturation is a good initial plan for broad populations unfamiliar with TIP. It is also important to reinforce and renew messages periodically so as not to lose the benefits of earlier efforts. However, USAID and other donors should consider whether at some point it is useful to develop post-saturation awareness strategies. Perhaps after mass outreach achieves and sustains an initial level of saturation across a country, mass outreach should be replaced, to a large degree, in subsequent phases of awareness campaigns, by a strong emphasis on targeting more refined techniques to transform people's attitudes and behaviors. General awareness activities would then be strategically planned (and monitored) to maintain high levels of message penetration in the population.

Another possible approach is to examine whether to combine more productively the expertise of those with substantive anti-trafficking experience with those from marketing and advertising professions who know how to craft and market effective messages. Generally, organizations working on human trafficking have developed awareness messages in-house and "marketed" those messages with little or no expert input in the techniques of identifying and reaching target audiences with messages created, tested, and targeted precisely for them. Advertising and marketing firms possess this specialized expertise. TIP awareness programs should seek to benefit from the experience of other successful awareness and prevention techniques from campaigns involving topics such as domestic violence and HIV/AIDS.[36] An initial inquiry should be made concerning what could be learned from these firms that would be directly applicable to producing more effective awareness prevention campaigns. In exploring how to make prevention more effective, implementing a trial partnership between firms with specialized marketing expertise and both local organizations and service providers would be useful.[37] Input into the crafting of prevention messages should be sought in appropriate ways as well from VoTs.

Tailor the Message to Magnify Its Impact

Many potential audiences exist for TIP awareness messages, and different audiences require messages adapted specificially for them to be most effective. Unfortunately, this is rarely done. Instead, awareness campaigns often look much the same regardless of the specifics of the country or the nature of the trafficking phenomenon therein (Limanowska, 2004:88).

Too often, a failure to differentiate and adapt content appropriately among even such core categories as children and adults has resulted. "On the whole, information campaigns aimed at children have drawn too much upon models used to target adult women" (Dottridge, n.d:50). In such circumstances, chance for success is scant. Minors and children "have a different way of seeing the world and because of this, adults are not always effective in their messages to them" (Surtees, 2006b:488). As a result, "[m]ore attention is needed to how minors see and understand messages and information."

Recent research reveals that to be most effective, anti-trafficking messages to men also need to be adjusted. Men may be resistent to being labeled as "victims" of trafficking, and thus messages using this type of language and content are less likely to resonate with them and elicit the results sought (Surtees, 2008a; 2008b:16-36; 2007:211-15).[38]

A bedrock of many awareness campaigns is to show the horrors of being trafficked. However, it now appears that the more sensationalized the image and frightening the message, the more unlikely that the general population will relate to it, thereby diminishing its potential for preventing TIP. An example of the disconnect between awareness and a sense of identification that could alter behavior occurred in Moldova. There, the film "Lilya-4-ever" was the centerpiece of a major awareness-raising campaign until it was discovered that people did not find similarities between their own experiences and that of the film's central character. Increasingly, scare tactics are considered ineffective as a prevention technique and may have unintended consequences, such as reinforcing stigma against VoTs (see e.g., Rosenberg, 2004:15).[39]

There is a need to precisely determine how different groups take in, process, digest, and act upon messages. A more systematic examination of these issues could pinpoint differences, perhaps to an unanticipated degree, among and within different age categories of children, ethnic minorities, religious groups, social groups, geographic locations, etc., that are not reached effectively using more generic or poorly designed anti-trafficking messages.

Research that provides the basis for tailoring messages should include input from the target groups. Messages targeting children, for example, should be tested with that age group before use. Prevention messages (as well as other aspects of prevention programs) can benefit from the input of former VoTs, as well. As a result, appropriate and ethical participation of former VoTs should be sought to elicit their first-hand perspectives in the program design process.

Sustained Employment Placement Is the Key to Economic-based Prevention

Employment programs addressing the absence of economic opportunity are a central part of anti-trafficking prevention work that is in high demand. Several large-scale USAID projects include this element. According to Winrock International, over 200,000 women in Ukraine, for example, have received services ranging from employment training, entrepreneurship courses to build marketable skills, leadership training, and trafficking prevention programming (Winrock, 2004:6). Course offerings are often over-subscribed.[40]

Employment programs typically focus on the supply side: helping women learn the skills needed to be more employable or prepared to start their own businesses. Employment and empowerment programs in the E&E region have had significant success in training and advising tens of thousands of women. Many participants report increases in confidence and self-esteem coupled with a sense of purpose and opportunity within their home communities.

One may conclude that individual participants and the larger community receive many important benefits from employment and empowerment programs; these benefits should be encouraged and supported by policymakers and donors, although it is not yet possible to establish a concrete causal link between these activities and prevention of trafficking.

As has been noted, training and personal development is only a means to an end. The key to improving the prevention impact of such programs is ensuring that, fairly quickly upon the conclusion of the course(s), participants are able to find jobs locally or sustain viable new local businesses that provide economic security for an extended period of time.

In the challenging environment existing in many countries of origin, these initiatives have had as much success as is reasonably possible in assisting graduates of their programs to get jobs. Nevertheless, despite numerous success stories region-wide, the evidence of local long-term employment for participants is scant. No longitudinal data have been gathered systematically to track graduates' continuing residences in a country after participating in a project, much less whether they have been trafficked.[41]

Monitoring job placement results over time is particularly important. Currently, programs tend to sample up to one third of their graduates three and six months after participation to determine whether they are seeking employment abroad. However, projects should be structured so as to gather data at least one year, and preferably longer, after the conclusion of the program in order to determine: 1) what participants' employment situations are; 2) whether or not they are employed locally and what their plans are (e.g., are they looking to go abroad for work or for other reasons?); and 3) to obtain valuable information on how to improve employment and income generation courses to be more helpful to participants in achieving financial security for themselves and their families.

Consideration should be given to increasing the sample size to include as close to all participants as practical and follow up with as many participants as possible (at a level of respondents greater than would be necessary to obtain reliable and useful follow-up data results) at six month intervals after that.

While generating this information may be challenging, it is critical for assessing prevention impact to go beyond statistics regarding initial job placement and for verifying whether employment has been maintained for at least twelve months, if not longer, even in cases where beneficiaries move through a series of job placements. Consequently, projects need to show indicators of sustained prevention success over time: six months, one year, and two years after initial placement.[42]

Individuals signing up for trainings could be requested to indicate a willingness in advance to participate in a follow-up survey about employment during the year subsequent to training in order to help document the success of the project. The pros and cons of making such a request for voluntary participation in the interest of improving a project's prevention efforts should be evaluated, but in the context of projects that are essentially offering courses to the general population of women, this may be useful and appropriate. Indeed, the collection and analysis of data from graduates probably could have been built into several current E&E projects as they are multi-year projects implemented by international organizations with well-established country presences.

Address Demand

Addressing the demand for trafficked individuals is an important component of United States policy and international standards. Campaigns that seek to reduce the demand for commercial sex and the demand for exploitable labor in sectors such as agriculture and construction in which trafficking may exist are intended, through these indirect means, to suppress incidences of TIP.

To date, the effectiveness of techniques aimed at demand reduction have not been analyzed systematically in the E&E region. Such evaluation will be important to provide governments with a better understanding and identification of which methods work and which do not and why.

Identifying the most effective demand reduction methods to reduce TIP would probably require a systematic country-by-country analysis to identify regional trends and patterns in demand for trafficked individuals over time. The importance of evaluating the effectiveness of these methods from a larger, regional perspective is that the prevention of trafficking based upon demand techniques presumes that there will be a reduction in overall trafficking and not simply the relocation of TIP from one place to other locations within the same country or to a different country (a phenomenon sometimes referred to as "push down, pop up").

Prevention in the Context of Gender

Significantly for prevention efforts, gender interacts with a number of the factors that are viewed as contributing to a heightened risk of trafficking in persons.[43] A prevalent perception that has been observed is that "men migrate, but women are trafficked." In other words, a bias that men may have bad migration experiences, but only women are trafficked persists. In any country where this perception is a prevailing view, either among government officials or the public in general, it will likely cause a compromising impact on prevention efforts. Therefore, it is important to understand if this type of bias exists in countries of the E&E region, and, if this misperception is found, a strategy should be developed to counteract it.[44]

RECOMMENDATIONS [45]

This section summarizes recommendations based upon the findings and analysis contained within the body of the text of this chapter. They are presented for the consideration and evaluation of those interested in improving the prevention efforts in the E&E region.

1. Donors and TIP prevention program implementers should **strengthen the understanding of underlying contributing factors in order to improve TIP prevention programming.**
   a. Analyze what type of data needs to be collected – and how it can be collected across the region – to form the basis of reliable empirical findings about root causes, contributing factors, risks, and vulnerabilities linked to TIP.
   b. Ascertain what factors work to counter vulnerabilities and risk of potential victims of TIP. Analyze what differentiates the circumstances of similarly situated individuals, some who are eventually trafficked and some are not.
2. Donors and TIP prevention program implementers should **refine the link between project activities and TIP prevention outcomes.**
   a. Gather new data for prevention results assessments.
   b. Develop long term frameworks within which individual TIP projects are located to permit determination of prevention results. Strategies should be developed, including post-project evaluation methods, to compensate for existing structural impediments (e.g., short-term, incremental projects) to accomplish this.
   c. Incorporate into future TIP projects data collection procedures that will permit evaluation by independent evaluators and researchers at points in time after the completion of the project.
   d. Design research projects to answer questions specific to establishing the link between TIP prevention activities and prevention results.
   e. Require monitoring and evaluation (M&E) to be an integral component of TIP prevention projects.
   f. Develop baselines and outcome indicators that are specific, meaningful, and measurable.
   g. Utilize impact evaluations to illustrate positive and negative results, as well as intended and unintended consequences.
   h. Fund the budget requirements for projects to implement sound M&E.
   i. Develop incentives for TIP prevention project applicants and/or implementers to initiate stronger outcome indicators for their respective projects to supplement and link to output measures.
   j. Supplement internal evaluation of TIP prevention projects with external evaluation work. Self-evaluation by project implementers, although useful for project management purposes and

for donors as part of a larger evaluation approach, is not a substitute for objective assessments by experienced researchers and evaluators.

3. Donors and TIP prevention program implementing organizations should work together to **refine their ability to target prevention programs to at-risk groups.**
    a. With more precision, identify and disaggregate groups at risk of being potential victims of TIP.
    b. Address all forms of trafficking in persons in implementation of TIP prevention strategies.
    c. Identify all populations underserved by TIP prevention projects for each country in the E&E region.
    d. Incorporate neglected at-risk groups into TIP prevention strategy development and program design. Strategies and projects should be adapted for these groups to be effective.
    e. Extend TIP prevention efforts to reach at-risk populations in rural communities more systematically.
    f. Examine opportunities to partner/collaborate with prevention-related projects provided by governments and NGOs, especially to expand ability to reach underserved populations and/or communities with TIP prevention efforts.
4. Donors and TIP prevention program implementing organizations should **prioritize TIP awareness-raising projects that emphasize prevention.**
    a. For projects in countries reporting extremely high levels of TIP awareness (i.e., awareness saturation) among the country's population, examine whether adjustments should be undertaken to improve prevention effectiveness rather than merely continuing the status quo of message saturation.
    b. Emphasize TIP awareness projects that employ methods that over time will demonstrate prevention results over information "campaigns" with general messages (with the exception of outreach to areas that still have little prior knowledge of TIP).
    c. Avoid sensationalized, alarmist, or frightening awareness messages. Scare tactics about TIP do not appear to resonate with intended recipients of those messages.
    d. Examine whether messages with information that provide ways for the individual to protect him/herself from falling victim to TIP lead to better prevention results than general messages.

e. Determine more precisely how different groups take in, process, digest, and act upon messages. Generic messages have dubious prevention value.
f. Magnify the impact of awareness/prevention messages by tailoring them more precisely to more targeted audiences.
g. Test prevention messages for effectiveness with minors of different age-groups. Assume that anti-TIP messages created for adults will not resonate effectively with children.
h. Revisit awareness messages for men and consider whether adjustments are necessary based upon resistance to the label of "victim" for TIP.
i. Consider whether experts in advertising and media message content can contribute to the development of awareness messages and strategies by TIP prevention projects.
j. Examine whether there are lessons to be learned from those experienced with awareness campaigns designed to change behavior or attitudes for issues such as domestic violence or HIV/AIDS.
k. To the extent appropriate and ethical, seek to include participation of former VoTs to elicit their first-hand perspectives in the design of TIP prevention projects.

5. Donors and TIP prevention program implementing organizations should **tighten the link between employment-based, income-generating, and empowerment prevention activities and long-term prevention results**
   a. Monitor job placement for graduates of economic-based courses over time. Continue documenting beyond initial job placement if necessary to evaluate prevention impact associated with sustained local employment. It is only over time (at least one year after the conclusion of the project) that prevention results can be assessed.
   b. Examine the effectiveness of achieving TIP prevention arising from skills training and empowerment programs within the context of local employment and economic conditions in each country of the E&E region. Review, for example, the extent to which graduates of these programs from economically suppressed areas ultimately migrate to other countries seeking employment and what happens to graduates who stay but do not find jobs.

   c. Conduct further research regarding tailoring the design of income-generating projects to serve TIP prevention objectives most effectively.

6. Donors and TIP prevention program implementing organizations should **ensure that safe migration projects supported by anti-TIP grants and contracts are tailored specifically to maximize achieving TIP prevention objectives**.
   a. Data gathering and analysis of safe migration TIP prevention projects need to be strengthened to identify factors and circumstances of program participants (apart from the criminal intervention of a trafficker) that differentiate an individual who migrates successfully from one who is trafficked. To start, data should be collected from assisted VoTs about whether they participated in safe migration projects prior to being trafficked and why, from their perspective, the content of those projects failed in preventing them from being trafficked.
   b. Examine whether cooperative partnerships can be developed between NGOs in countries of origin and those in countries of destination in order to vet jobs in destination countries. Consideration could also be given to whether job vetting is a prevention approach for which government-NGO collaborations could be developed.
7. Donors and TIP prevention program implementing organizations should **include demand reduction approaches** that demonstrate effective TIP prevention results as part of comprehensive TIP prevention strategy.
   a. Address demand reduction as part of comprehensive TIP prevention strategies.
   b. Conduct the first analysis of the **effectiveness of demand** as a prevention method for different forms of TIP.
8. Donors and TIP prevention program implementing organizations should **consider TIP prevention impact of gender-based factors.**
   a. Determine if gender stereotypes about who is likely to be a TIP victim and preconceptions hamper TIP prevention efforts.

ANNEX A. REFERENCES

AED-SARI/Equity Team. n.d. *Prevention of Trafficking and Protection of Victims of Violence – Replicable Approaches: A Guide*. Washington, DC: The Academy for Educational Development.

Anderson, Bridget and Julia O'Connell Davidson. (2004*). Trafficking: A Demand Led Problem? Save the Children*, Sweden.

———. (2003). *Is Trafficking in Human Beings Demand Driven? A Multi-County Pilot Study*. Geneva: IOM.

Animus Association Foundation. (2004). *Annual Report of "Animus Association" Foundation for 2004*. Bulgaria.

Aradau, Claudia. (2005). *Good Practices in Response to Trafficking in Human Beings*. Danish Red Cross.

ASTRA. (2005). ASTRA SOS Hotline and Direct Victim Assistance. Belgrade (document on file at NEXUS Institute library).

ASTRA. (2002-2003). *Biannual Report*. Belgrade.

ASTRA. n.d. *Trafficking in Women – Manual for Journalists*. CIDA.

Bales, Kevin. (2005). Understanding Global Slavery: A Reader. *Berkeley/Los Angeles:* University of California Press:

Bales, Kevin. (1999). Disposable People: New Slavery in the Global Economy. *Berkeley/Los Angeles*: University of California Press.

Bedekbayeva, Aidai. (2005). *Preventing Human Trafficking in Kyrgyzstan Project: Project Evaluation Report*. Winrock International.

Blumberg, Rae Lesser & Olha Shved. (2002). *Curbing Sex Slavery Abroad by Helping Women Earn a Living in Ukraine: An Assessment of the Economic Empowerment Aspects of the Anti-Trafficking Project*. USAID Kiev, DAI, Inc., and USAID Office of Women in Development.

Boak, Alison, Amy Boldosser & Ofronama Biu, eds. (2003). *Smooth Flight: A Guide to Preventing Youth Trafficking*. International Organization for Adolescents. Brooklyn: New York.

Bott, Sarah, Andrew Morrison & Mary Ellsberg. (2005). *Preventing and Responding to Gender-based Violence in Middle and Low Income Countries: A Global Review and Analysis*. World Bank.

Brunovskis, Anette & Rebecca Surtees. (2007). *Leaving the Past Behind? When Victims of Trafficking Decline Assistance*. Oslo: Fafo Institute and Vienna: NEXUS Institute.

Brunovkis, Anette & Guir Tyldum. (2004). *Crossing Borders: An Empirical Study of Transnational Prostitution and Trafficking in Human Beings*. Norway: Fafo Institute.

Bugnion, Christian. (2008). *Presentation from ARTIP M&E Workshop*. Subur Consulting (material available from NEXUS Institute library files).

CAII. (2007). *The State of Efforts to Combat Trafficking in Persons in Albania – August 2006-July 2007*. Washington, DC: Creative Associates International, Inc.

Callender, Elizabeth, Theresa Esquibel, Rebecca Sewall & Anne Zollner. (2003). *Mid-term Evaluation of the USDOL/IREX Regional Empowerment Initiative for Women, November 2002 – February 2003*. Washington, DC: Management Systems International.

Catholic Relief Services. (2003). *Trafficking of Roma Women and Children from Serbia – Risk and Resiliency Factors*. CRS Serbia & Montenegro Program: CRS.

Centre for Urban & Regional Research (CURS), Institute for Life Quality Research (ILQR), and MERCURY Research and Marketing Consultants. n.d. Vulnerability to Trafficking in Human Beings of Young Female Population in Romania (excerpt on file at NEXUS Institute library).

De Sas Kropiwnicki, Zosa. (2007). *Children Speak Out: Trafficking Risk and Resilience in Southeast Europe*. Save the Children in Albania.

Dottridge, Mike. (2007a). *Measuring Responses to Trafficking in Human Beings in the European Union— An Assessment Manual (Draft Text)*. Brussels: European Commission.

———. (2007b). "*The Role of Research in Preventing Human Trafficking and Identifying People Being Trafficked*." Remarks presented at Alliance Against Trafficking in Persons conference, "Assistance to Trafficked Persons: We Can Do Better." Vienna (on file at NEXUS Institute library).

———. (2007c). *A Handbook on Planning Projects to Prevent Child Trafficking*. Lausanne: Terre des Hommes Foundation.

———. (2004). *Kids as Commodities: Child Trafficking and What to Do about It*. Lausanne: International Federation Terre des Hommes.

———. n.d. *Action to Prevent Child Trafficking in South Eastern Europe: A Preliminary Assessment*. Terre des Hommes/UNICEF.

GAO. (2006). *Human Trafficking: Better Data, Strategy, and Reporting Needed to Enhance U.S. Anti-trafficking Efforts Abroad*. Washington DC: General Accountability Office.

GAO. (2007). *Human Trafficking: Monitoring and Evaluation of International Projects Are Limited, but Experts Suggest Improvements*. Washington, DC: General Accountability Office.

GAO. (2007). *Human Trafficking: A Strategic Framework Could Help Enhance the Interagency Process*. Washington, DC: General Accountability Office..

GAATW. (2007). *Collateral Damage: The Impact of Anti-Trafficking Measures on Human Rights around the World*. Bangkok: GAATW.

Gimon M., Kazi N., Mikhail D., Mueller J., Ryan P. & Stoehr K. (2003). *Not for Sale: Child Trafficking Prevention in South Eastern Europe. New York:* UNICEF/Columbia University.

GYLA. (2007). Quarterly Report: April 1, 2007 – June 30, 2007 for Program Title: No to Trafficking in Persons. USAID Cooperative Agreement # 114-A-00-05-00107. Tbilisi: Georgia Young Lawyers Association.

GfK Ukraine. (2006). Human Trafficking Survey: Belarus, Bulgaria, Moldova, Romania, and Ukraine.

ICMC Croatia. (2003). Victims Assistance and Protection Program for Women Rescued from Trafficking. Final Report, submitted to USAID. Zagreb: International Catholic Migration Commission.

IHF. (2001). Trafficking in Women: Innovative Strategies and Tools for Action, Final Conference Report. Vienna: International Helsinki Federation for Human Rights and La Strada International.

IHF. (2001). Presentation of Eleanor Valentine, Winrock International, Trafficking Program Director. Kyiv.

Institute of Pedagogical Studies & IOM. (2003). Trafficking in Human Beings and the Role of the School in Its Prevention. Tirana: IOM.

———. (2003). *Trafficking in Human Beings and the Role of the School in its Prevention: Manual for Teachers*. Tirana: IOM.

———. (2003). *Trafficking in Human Beings and the Role of the School in its Prevention: For the Basic School Pupils*. Tirana: IOM.

International Labor Organization (ILO). n.d. Trafficking and Forced Labour: Monitoring Recruitment - Training Manual for Trainers (publication information unavailable).

———. (2005). *Tools for Prevention – Participatory Monitoring: Guidelines for Practitioners in the Fight against Human Trafficking*. Bangkok: ILO.

IOM. (2008). *Quarterly Report to USAID on Prevention of Trafficking in Persons in Belarus*, October 1December 31, 2007. IOM.

———. (2007a). *Q4 Year 3 Quarterly Report to USAID Countering Trafficking in Persons in Ukraine*. Ukraine: IOM.

———. (2007b). *Combating Trafficking in Human Beings in Ukraine: Statistics – Updated on March 31, 2007*. Ukraine: IOM.

———. (2006a). *Annual Report to USAID on Prevention of Trafficking in Persons in Belarus*. IOM.

———. (2006b). *Human Trafficking Survey: Belarus, Bulgaria, Moldova,*

Romania, and Ukraine, December 2006. Kyiv: International Organization for Migration.

———. (2006c). *Final Report of IOM's Counter-Trafficking Activities Funded by USAID Montengro. October 1 2002-March 7, 2006.* Podgoica: IOM.

———. (2005a). *IOM Quarterly Report for the Period from 01 January to 31 March 2005.* Hotline Statistics – Central Asia.

———. (2005b). *Final Report: Prevention and Awareness-Raising Campaign on Trafficking in Bosnia and Herzegovina.* Sarajevo: IOM.

———. (2005c). Interim Report to the U.S. Agency for International Development and the Swedish Agency for International Development (SIDA): Combating Trafficking in Persons in Central Asia, April 1- June 30, 2005. Almaty: International Organization for Migration.

———. (2005d). The Problem of Human Trafficking in Uzbekistan.

———. (2002). Report on the Nationwide Survey Conducted on Attitudes of Albanian Teenagers on Migration and Trafficking in Human Beings. Tirana: IOM.

———. n.d. Trafficking As It Is: A Statistical Profile Update 2000-2006.

———. n.d. Project Description. Bulgaria.

IREX. (2006). Anti-Trafficking and Information Dissemination (TPID): Final Report, April 2003-February 2006. Washington D.C: IREX.

Kelly, Elizabeth. (2002). *Journeys of Jeopardy: Current Research on Trafficking of Women and Children for Sexual Exploitation in Europe.* Geneva: IOM.

Kelly, Liz. (2005). *Fertile Fields: Trafficking in Persons in Central Asia.* Vienna: IOM.

La Strada International. Belarus website: *http://www.lastradainter national.org/?main=l*astradaoffices&section=belarus

La Strada International. (2008). *Violation of Women's Rights: A Cause and Consequence of Trafficking in Women.* Amsterdam: La Strada International.

Lazaroiu, Sebastian & Monica Alexandru. (2003). *Who Is the Next Victim? Vulnerability of Young Romanian Women to Trafficking in Human Beings.* Romania: IOM.

———. (2004). Internal Trafficking in Romania. Bucharest: IOM.

Limanowska, Barbara. (2005). *Trafficking in Human Beings in South Eastern Europe: Focus on Prevention.* UNICEF, UNOHCHR, and OSCE/ODIHR.

———. (2003). *Trafficking in Human Beings in South Eastern Europe: 2003 Update on Situation and Responses to Trafficking in Human Beings.*

UNICEF, UNOHCHR, and OSCE/ODIHR.

Office of the Coordinator of U.S. Assistance to the NIS. Report to Congress on Efforts to Combat Domestic Violence and Trafficking in Russia, Ukraine, Moldova and Central Asia: Summary of USAID Activities. Washington, DC.

Marshall, Phil. (2005). *Raising Our Own Awareness: Getting to Grip with Trafficking in Persons and Related Problems in South-East Asia and Beyond. Asia-Pacific Population Journa*l, December.

Mendelson, Sarah. (2005). *Barracks and Brothels: Peacekeepers and Human Trafficking in the Balkans*. Washington, DC: CSI Press.

Ministry of Education of the Republic of Moldova, UNICEF, Radda Barnen (Swedish Save the Children) & Child Rights Information Center. (2004). Evaluation Report: Life Skills Education for Prevention of Trafficking in Human Beings. Moldova: UNICEF.

Nunez, Manuel, Gladkyy Oleksandr, Yaroslav Yurtsaba & Timothy J. Tappe. (2005). *Labor Market Assessment in Ten Selected Oblasts of Ukraine: Averting the Negative Effects of Outward Labor Migration and Human Trafficking by Improving the Economic Situation*. European Union.

Omelaniuk, Irena. (2005). *Trafficking in Human Beings. Paper for United Nations Expert Group Meeting on International Migration and Development*. New York.

Orfano, Isabella. (2007). *Overview on the Phenomenon of Human Traffic at National Level*. EU: Headway.

OSCE Office of Democratic Institutions and Human Rights. (2006). *Awareness Raising for Roma Activists on the Issue of Trafficking in Human Beings in South-Eastern Europe*. Warsaw: OSCE.

OSCE, UNICEF, USAID, and British Council and Ukraine Ministry of Family, Children & Youth. (2004). Trafficking in Ukraine: An Assessment of Current Responses.

Pojman, Ruth & Tatiana Timoshenko. (2007). *Assessment of the USAID/Belarus IOM Anti-Trafficking Program*. Washington, DC: USAID.

PRISM. (2007). *Research Study on Trafficking in Human Beings. Partnership against Trafficking in Human Beings*. Kosovo: Prism Research.

Rende Taylor, Lisa. (2005). Dangerous Trade-offs: The Behavioral Ecology of Child Labor and Prostitution in Rural Northern Thailand. *Current Anthropology*, *46(3)*.

Rosenberg, Ruth. (2008). *Best Practice for Programming to Protect and Assist Victims of Trafficking in Europe and Eurasia*. Washington, DC: Creative

Assoc./JBS Aguirre International.

———. (2004). *Best Practices for Programming to Prevent Trafficking in Human Beings in Europe and Eurasia*. Bethesda, MD: Development Alternatives, Inc. and USAID.

Rudd, Jane. (2001). *A Report on Trafficking Prevention Efforts in Ukraine: Impact of the Women for Women Centers on At-risk Teen and Adult Centers*. Winrock International and USAID.

———. (2002). *Summary Report of Trafficking of Women in Ukraine*. Winrock International and USAID.

Snajdrova, Hana & Blanka Hanilova. (2007). *Trafficking in Human Beings in the Republic of Armenia*. Yerevan: OSCE.

Somach, Susan. n.d. Assessment of IREX's Trafficking Prevention and Information Dissemination (TPID) Program. Washington, DC: International Research & Exchanges Board.

Somach, Susan and Rebecca Surtees. (2005). Albania Anti-trafficking Evaluation October 24-December 19, 2005. Washington, DC:USAID.

Stojovic Jankovic, Ana. (2004). *Stealing the Childhood: Combating Child Trafficking in Montenegro*. Montenegro: Save the Children.

Surtees, Rebecca. (2008a). *Trafficking of Men: A Trend Less Considered: The Case of Belarus and Ukraine*. IOM Global Database Thematic Research Series Geneva. Geneva: IOM.

———. (2008b). *Trafficked Men as Unwilling Victims. St. Antony's International Review*, 2000, *14(1)*.

———. (2008c). *Handbook on Anti-Trafficking Data Collection in South-Eastern Europe: Developing Regional Criteria*. Vienna: ICMPD.

———. (2007). *Listening to Victims: Experiences of Identification, Return and Assistance in South-Eastern Europe*. Vienna: ICMPD.

———. (2006a). *Building the Capacity of Roma Communities to Combat Trafficking in Human Beings: Roundtable Report*, Planners of prevention methodology should study in detail re-trafficking cases more closely to determine what lessons can be extracted to be applied to awareness programs aimed at those who have never been trafficked. Warsaw: ODIHR.

———. (2006b). Child Trafficking: Different Forms of Trafficking & Alternative Interventions. *Tulane Journal of International & Comparative Law, 14 (2)*.

———. (2005). *Second Annual Report on Victim of Trafficking in South Eastern Europe*. Geneva: IOM.

———. (2004). *Regional Clearing Point: Annotated Guide to Internet-Based*

Counter-Trafficking Resources. IOM

———. n.d. Monitoring and Evaluating Reintegration Work – Developing Indicators for TVRP in SEE. Discussion Paper #2, Trafficking Victims Reintegration Programme (TVRP) in South-Eastern Europe. An initiative of the King Baudouin Foundation (available from NEXUS Institute library).

Terre des Hommes. (2008). TACT 3 – Quarterly Reports Nos. 5-7. June 2007-February 2008. Tirana.

———. (2007). TACT 3 – Yearly Report June 2006-June 207. Tirana.

———. (2006). TACT II Final Report May 2003-2006. Tirana.

Terre des Homes & Ndihme Per Femijet. (2005). *Child Trafficking in South Eastern Europe: The Development of Good Practices to Protect Albanian Children*. USAID, UNICEF, SIdA, and Oak Foundation.

Timoshenko, Tatiana. (2005). *Countering Trafficking in Persons in Ukraine (a power point presentation)*. Ukraine: USAID (copy on file at NEXUS Institute library).

Tschanz, M. (2001). *Case Study on the Impact of Information Campaigns. IOM in Eastern Europe and Central Asia* (Newsletter), Issue 3, April-June.

Tyuryukanova, Elena. (2006). *Human Trafficking in the Russian Federation: Inventory and Analysis of the Current Situation and Responses*. Moscow: Institute for Urban Economics.

———. (2005). *Forced Labour in the Russian Federation Today: Irregular Migration and Trafficking in Human Beings*. Geneva: ILO.

Tozaj, Dolor. (2006). *The State of Efforts to Combat Trafficking in Persons in Albania – January 2005 to July 2006: An Overview of Governmental and Civil Society Policies and Programs*. Washington, DC: USAID.

Shinkle, Whitney. (2007). *Preventing Human Trafficking: An Evaluation of Current Efforts*. Institute for the Study of International Migration. Washington, DC: Walsh School of Foreign Service and Georgetown University.

Social Monitoring Center & Ukrainian Institute of Social Studies. (2001). Nationwide Survey: Trafficking in Women as a Social Problem in Ukrainian Society. Summary of Findings. USAID and Winrock International.

United Nations. (2004). Human Trafficking Resource Package Department of Peacekeeping Operations. New York.

———. (2000). Report of the Special Rapporteur on Violence Against Women, Its Causes and Consequences, Ms. Radhika Coomaraswamy, On

Trafficking in Women, Women's Migration and Violence against Women. Submitted in accordance with Commission on Human Rights resolution 1997/44. New York.

UNODC. (2006). *Tool Kit to Combat Trafficking in Persons*. Vienna: United Nations.

UNIAP SIREN. (2007). *Targeting Endemic Vulnerability Factors to Human Trafficking*. Bangkok: UNIAP.

UNICEF. (2006). *Children on the Brink: A Focused Situation Analysis of Vulnerable, Excluded and Discriminated Children in Romania*.

———. (2002). *The Situation of Children and Family in the Republic of Moldova*. Moldova: UNICEF.

———. (2008). *Child Trafficking in Europe: A Broad Vision to Put Children First. Innocenti Research Centre*. Florence: UNICEF IRC.

USAID. (2007). *Briefing Paper: USAID Anti-Trafficking Activities in Moldova*. Winrock International, UNDP, and USAID, May 2007.

———. (2006). *Trafficking in Persons: USAID Response*. Washington, DC: USAID.

U.S. Department of State. (2008). *U.S. Government Efforts to Fight Demand Fueling Human Trafficking*. Washington, DC: Office to Monitor and Combat Trafficking in Persons.

Warnath, Stephen. (2007). *Examining the Intersection Between Trafficking in Persons and Domestic Violence*. Washington, DC: Creative Associates/Aguirre Division of JBS International Inc.

Watson, Charlotte. (2005a). *Trafficking in Persons Assessment Kazakhstan*. USAID CAR, June 2005.

———. (2005b). *Trafficking in Persons Assessment Kyrgyzstan*. USAID CAR, June 2005.

———. (2005c). *Trafficking in Persons Assessment Tajikistan*. USAID CAR, June 2005.

———. (2005d). *Trafficking in Persons Assessment Uzbekistan*. USAID CAR, June 2005.

Winrock International. Winning Strategies: Trafficking Prevention Project in the Ukraine 1998-2004. Arkansas: Winrock International.

———. (2007). Anti-Trafficking Initiative in Moldova – New Perspectives for Women: First Quarterly Progress Report for 2007.

———. (2004a). Third & Final Quarterly Progress Report, Year Six: Trafficking Prevention Project in Ukraine, January - April 2004.

———. (2004b). Final Report: Prevention of Trafficking in Women through Expansion of Economic Opportunities in Belarus.

Winrock PMEP. n.d. Winrock Performance Monitoring and Evaluation Plan. Moldova: Winrock.

Winrock. Moldova website: www.winrock.org/md.

Winrock. Russia website: www.success.winrock.ru.

Wolfensohn, Galit. (2004). Responding to Child Trafficking: An Introductory Handbook to Child Rights-based Interventions Drawn from Save the Children's Experiences in Southeast Europe. Albania: Save the Children.

Women for Future. (2003). *Trafficking of Women and Girls in Georgia: Sociological Survey.*

End Notes

[1] Rosenberg, Ruth. "Best Practices for Programming to Prevent Trafficking in Human Beings in Europe and Eurasia." USAID/Development Alternatives, Inc., September 2004.

[2] For simplicity of language, Bosnia and Herzegovina will be referred to as Bosnia or BiH.

[3] This has since been renamed the Office of the Undersecretary for Democracy and Global Affairs.

[4] The functions of the USIA were folded into the Department of State's Bureau of Public Affairs by law in 1999.

[5] A comprehensive introduction to prevention project approaches is provided by Rosenberg (2004).

[6] See Rosenberg (2004).

[7] See La Strada Belarus website (referring to need to change prevailing attitudes that stigmatize trafficking victims as perpetrators, prostitutes, illegal immigrants, or "bad people who come to a country and spread sexually transmitted diseases").

[8] This information is distilled from GYLA, 2007.

[9] In the E&E region, one of the most ambitious uses of a school-based awareness raising is the TACT program in Albania. The reported output measures suggest the scope of this project: *Through 2170 awareness raising sessions organized in 70 schools of 14 districts of Albania, 35711 schoolchildren have been informed through a first round of prevention, while 22549 children have benefited from a refresher kit of prevention. The total number of impacted children has been 58 260 . . . There have been, in total, 69 awareness raising sessions organized with 1507 teachers and 139 headmasters.* (TdH, 2006)

Educational programs have been conducted in other countries in the E&E region, including Ukraine, Russia, and Romania. By 2004, educational programs on trafficking for school children had been included in all National Plans of Action in the countries of Southeast Europe (Limanowska, 2005:83).

[10] Rosenberg (2004) reported evidence provided by NGOs of increases in awareness in several other countries in the E&E region: in Croatia, following a series of seminars for law enforcers, judges, lawyers, and prosecutors, participants showed a 20 percent increase in their understanding of trafficking (Rosenberg, 2004 citing ICMC Croatia, 2003). A study in Georgia "demonstrated a fivefold increase in the general population's understanding of trafficking following a concerted information campaign" ("Women for Future"). In 2001, prior to the campaign start, only 20 percent of respondents associated trafficking with sexual exploitation, while a second study conducted two years later, found that 100 percent of the respondents knew that sexual exploitation is a form of trafficking. The study also cited other examples of the increased knowledge of the population in the past two years.

The authors attribute this increase to the awareness-raising campaigns conducted in the interim.

[11] An earlier study in Ukraine (see Rudd, 2002) found that 38 percent of the general population knew about the dangers of trafficking. A presentation by USAID Ukraine in 2005 reported that 99 percent of 1048 respondents surveyed in Ukraine had an understanding of the problem (Timoshenko 2005:4). Overall, the data suggest that efforts to raise awareness have been effective over time.

[12] Other recent research in Belarus suggests even higher levels of awareness. It found that the number of people aware of the TIP phenomenon had increased from 96 percent in 2006 to 98 percent in 2007 (IOM, 2007).

[13] Programs of employment-related training and placement serve prevention objectives for "potential" victims and help guard against the re-trafficking of returned victims. They also serve recovery purposes for VoTs.

[14] Also, 141 trafficking victims (presumably returned to Moldova, although perhaps some internally trafficked victims) received assistance services (Winrock International & UNDP, 2007).

[15] Whether detailed research has been done regarding how the various camps in countries in the E&E region complement, duplicate, or overlap with each other is unclear. A more effective use of resources may involve determining whether a human trafficking awareness component can be incorporated into other "non-trafficking" summer camps and other empowerment programs by working co-operatively or in joint partnership.

[16] The TACT project uses the term "children at risk" to refer to "children directly exposed" to the risk of being trafficked (usually children under exploitation by their families but not moved, brothers or sisters of victims, or children intercepted just before being trafficked) (TdH 2006, fn.1). It uses the term "suspected victims" to refer to "children exploited in the streets (for forced begging, forced labor or in less extend [sic] sexual exploitation) and moved across borders or internally for the purpose of exploiting them" (id.).

[17] It would be interesting to know more than this project's anecdote permits about the facts on which the women based their suspicions that the other women they met had been trafficked. Because the grounds for their suspicions are not elaborated and other factors, although suspicious, are not conclusive, it is impossible to assess from the details of this illustration whether the young women avoided a trafficking danger or something less sinister. In any event, they remained safe. It also is unclear from this whether the womens' experience led to the company being reported, investigated, and prosecuted or what became of the other women.

[18] In 2003, the *Prosecutorial Remedies and Other Tools to End the Exploitation of Children Today Act (PROTECT) and the Trafficking Victims Protection Reauthorization Act* strengthened U.S. law that addressed the demand side of sex trafficking and other forms of sexual exploitation. The 2005 *Trafficking Victims Protection Reauthorization Act* also contains provisions directed at the demand side of labor trafficking, forced labor, and child labor.

In addition, Article 9 (5) of the Palermo Protocol obligates countries to discourage demand as one of their prevention tools:

State Parties shall adopt or strengthen legislative and other measures, such as educational, social or cultural measures, including through bilateral and multilateral cooperation, to discourage the demand that fosters exploitation of persons, especially women and children, that leads to trafficking.

[19] The scope of this project's work to achieve demand-side legal and social changes includes: Albania, Bulgaria, Croatia, the Czech Republic, Estonia, Hungary, Kosovo, Latvia, Lithuania, Moldova, Montenegro, Poland, Russia, and Serbia.

[20] As a general matter, one must be cautious about inferring too much about causation based upon observations about apparent changes in TIP levels or patterns. In the E&E, variables such as new membership in the EU and the Schengen agreement, for example, may have an impact

on TIP routes and patterns in ways that are not yet understood. Also, to determine whether TIP has declined overall in a community or country, it is necessary to ascertain whether transnational trafficking involving foreign women may have been offset by increases in internal trafficking.

21 Previous USAID-sponsored research indicates that VoTs appreciate that their perspectives and opinions were sought (Surtees, 2007:22).

22 "This term 'root causes' has become a buzz word in various anti-trafficking circles and yet there have been few attempts to define what is meant by this term or how it can be conceptualized and researched" (De Sas Kropiwnicki 2007:19).

23 Several research analysts have commented on the superficial nature of most discussions of root causes. For example: "Less sophisticated analyses tend to highlight the issue of poverty, which is seen to propel women into accepting dubious offers of employment. Even at the level of the supply, this oversimplifies the reality" (Kelly, 2002); "Academics and policymakers must move beyond 'poverty' and 'lack of education' to recognize the subtleties of the challenges and frustrations confronting people living in the less developed parts of our rapidly developing world" (Rende Taylor, 2005).

24 The only constant in all cases of TIP is the necessary intervention of a criminal agent – the trafficker(s).

25 Callender et al., observed: "To complicate matters further, the push and pull factors that contribute to the phenomenon [of trafficking] are highly subjective as individuals weigh the decision to seek employment abroad against their real or perceived benefits of staying within their communities . . . As such, efforts to combat trafficking usually demand a precise knowledge of the factors that influence the decision making processes for a specific target group and how these factors mesh with options available at the local level. This makes the design of any anti-trafficking initiative labor and time intensive and largely specific to each target group." (See also Surtees, 2005 regarding the subjective nature of perceptions about an individual's context and conditions and the desire and decision to migrate.).

26 Consider two examples of the how the prospects for achieving prevention objectives intersect with the decision-making process. The effectiveness of interventions may be undermined, for example, if programs fail to reach individuals in rural communities before they make their decision to leave their homes and families to migrate. Information obtained after the decision to migrate has been made (e.g., brochures in bus and train waiting areas) is less likely to reverse an individual's commitment to a course of action already set in motion and witnessed by family and friends. It is thus important to consider whether prevention activities are in sync with critical decision points.

As important as understanding the prevention implications of the timing of decisions is understanding who is involved or may influence decisions. While prevention strategies typically are directed toward an individual's decision to migrate, in many societies major economic decisions, such as decisions to migrate to improve economic circumstances (e.g., through remittances), are made on the household level (Brunovskis & Tyldum, 2004) rather than by the individual alone. Accordingly, examination of when and how decisions are made in households would inform development of good programming practices.

27 A discussion of the challenges of transforming the identification of factors that may counter-balance risks into insights for specific prevention strategies is found in De Sas Kropiwnicki (2007).

28 Nevertheless, a solid case can be made that family violence should be targeted in anti-trafficking prevention programs based upon the potential intersection between family violence and trafficking. Family violence may heighten an individual's vulnerability to being trafficked in three principal ways: 1) by creating an urgent need to seek an escape; 2) by eroding an individual's self-esteem and self-confidence; and 3) in combination with other factors, such as economic crisis, by serving as a tipping point to push an individual into action that leads to being trafficked. But this policy and operational decision must be

based upon a judgment concerning the potential intersection for now and not because family violence has not been established empirically as a clear "cause" of individuals being trafficked (Warnath, 2007; Lazaroiu & Alexandru, 2003; Rosenberg, 2004).

[29] And, contrary to common stereotypes about victim profiles, some VoTs held college degrees (Surtees, 2004).

[30] While it is true that virtually anyone can be "at-risk" of becoming a VoT, there are practicial implications for trying to address the large population pools of such broad categories. Young women and girls are an appropriate category to address because of the general risk to them of being trafficked. However, in larger countries, at least, it may be problematic to consider this group without some further disaggregation as a target category in any useful sense. In the Ukraine, for example, there are over 5 million 12 to 30-year-old women and girls (IHF 2001:36).

[31] The quality of risk assessment in devising target groups for prevention projects is unclear. During a USAID assessment of TIP programs in Russia, for example, Somach (2007) asked project implementers to define who was "at risk" for trafficking in their areas. The report found: "With a few notable exceptions . . . the definitions [of who was "at-risk"] were based primarily on media stories and training information they had received."

[32] IOM Bulgaria, for example, noted the large number of minorities who become VoTs in Bulgaria (IOM, "Project Description: Bulgaria" n.d.). It was reported that 81.8 percent of victims of trafficking for delinquency and begging in 2004 were Roma. For VoTs for sexual exploitation, minorities also comprised a significant share, with 42.6 percent in 2004. Roma made up 33.6 percent of victims of trafficking for sexual exploitation, Turks were 7.4 percent, and Pomaks were 1.6 percent. Surtees (2005:60 fn. 53) provides a review of Roma and Egyptian ethnicity among trafficking victims in Albania.

[33] For example, a USAID assessment conducted in Russia (Somach 2007) identified possible target groups who would not fall within common notions of potential VoTs but who were also vulnerable to being trafficked there. This included certain groups of men over 40, such as sailors traveling internationally at sea and selected groups of women over 40 from certain regions traveling abroad for housekeeping jobs (Somach 2007:18).

[34] The U.S. Government Accountability Office observed that the lack of an overall coordinated strategy capable of bringing together discrete anti-trafficking efforts across and within the departments and agencies of the U.S. Government into a more unified, coherent and comprehensive vision creates the risk of fragmentation that may waste scarce funds and limit program effectiveness (GAO, 2006:21-23). This chapter supported the importance of overcoming the limitations of piecemeal time-bound efforts to look instead at projects in terms of how each one fits into the larger context of continuing national anti-trafficking strategic objectives. Thus, a longer-term, holistic perspective is needed that cuts across the work of individual TIP prevention projects to enable each project in the USAID portfolio of prevention projects to be located within a larger strategic picture geographically and over time.

[35] See Bugnion (2008).

[36] Dottridge (n.d.:50) describes the value of drawing upon lessons learned from those conducting awareness campaigns to reach and influence children in other fields: "Many lessons can be taken from related fields such as advertising, advocacy and public health on how to run awareness campaigns that positively influence children."

[37] Since marketing firms typically have no in-house expertise in human trafficking, it would be counterproductive to try to utilize message experts unless there is a strong substantive involvement by trafficking experts.

[38] And it can be problematic for women as well to be so identified (Brunovskis & Surtees 2007: 135-147). Indeed, further consideration should be given to whether to use the term "victim," which probably is useful in policy-level discussions to underscore that men and women who have been trafficked are not criminals themselves but may have more limitations than previously realized for prevention.

[39] Awareness raising campaigns should consider when prevention objectives might be served by shifting to more specific messages, such as providing concrete information to help individuals protect themselves.

[40] Winrock reports that they had thousands of women on the waiting lists for some of their trainings.

[41] Empowerment programs face similar challenges to document/link cause and effect (even roughly) of project activities to prevention results.

[42] Realizing sustained economic opportunity is a minimum but not conclusive indicator of possible prevention impact. Note that Winrock International reports that approximately 40 percent of the clients at Women for Women Centers were already employed (Winrock International, 2004:5), so research regarding the prevention impact of participation needs to consider additional variables as well.

[43] "[T]he lack of rights afforded to women serves as the primary causative factor at the root of both women's migration and trafficking in women [. . .] By failing to protect and promote women's civil, political, economic and social rights, Governments create situations in which trafficking flourishes" (United Nations, 2000:54).

[44] Trafficking prevention would be strengthened if prevention measures were integrated into each country's gender (as well as economic, education, and social development) strategies and initiatives.

[45] The recommendations presented in Rosenberg (2004) remain useful and timely. This chapter incorporates those recommendations and, to the extent that they have not been enacted, renews the call for their implementation.

In: Human Trafficking in Europe and… ISBN: 978-1-61122-913-4
Editors: Charles R. Scott et al. © 2011 Nova Science Publishers, Inc.

Chapter 2

BEST PRACTICES FOR PROGRAMMING TO PROTECT AND ASSIST VICTIMS OF TRAFFICKING IN EUROPE AND EURASIA*

United States Agency for International Development

ACKNOWLEDGMENTS

My sincerest wish is that this chapter will result in better programs to support victims of trafficking throughout the region. I hope that the report and annexes provide a useful tool for developing improved programs for assisting victims of trafficking and for monitoring existing programs. The author is grateful to all of those whose work is referenced throughout the report and in Annex A. Without these informative reports, this assessment would not have been possible. The author sends thanks to the many USAID Mission employees throughout the region who made these materials available for this chapter. The author would also like to thank Rebecca Surtees from the Nexus Institute for her insightful comments on the draft report and provision of numerous useful resources for the report. And, finally, I would like to thank Catherine Cozzarelli from USAID, Ruth Pojman from OSCE, Christine Allison from the Aguirre Division of JBS International, Inc., and Sylvia

* This is an edited, reformatted and augmented edition of a United States Agency For International Development publication, dated November 2008.

Ellison from Creative Associates International, Inc., for their invaluable support and encouragement throughout.

I. Executive Summary

The report that follows is an assessment of trafficking protection programs – programs designed to provide protection and assistance to victims of trafficking. It is intended to help USAID and other interested parties determine the strengths and weaknesses of program approaches to date, ascertain which projects are replicable and where anti-TIP efforts can be integrated into other relevant USAID programming. A companion report has been written to assess trafficking prevention programs.

The report stems from a review of current literature produced by various USAID anti-TIP activities, and publicly accessible and relevant assessments and evaluations from anti-TIP programs funded by other donors (for a complete list, see Annex A, References). Additionally, the author draws on some of her own experiences in implementing anti-trafficking programs in countries of the region. One of the main limitations which was revealed by the use of this methodology was the dearth of impact data available in the existing literature and project documents. Project documents were found to contain mostly process or output indicators (numbers of people trained or assisted, for example). While the general objectives and goals of the projects were provided in the project documents, measurements of the impact of the projects were generally not provided or were not clear or specific enough to demonstrate program impact.

While there was a dearth of concrete indicators available which measured the impact of protection programs in the region, there was enough information to come to the conclusion that without the efforts of the USAID-funded anti-trafficking programs in the region, it is likely that victims of trafficking would rarely be identified, their human rights would continue to be violated, and few would be willing to testify without support and protection. Similarly, our understanding of trafficking in the region would be severely limited. We have learned much over the years from the victims who have been assisted through donor-funded programs. Without this information we would still be laboring under misconceptions about trafficking, its victims and the perpetrators.

This chapter provides an analytical review of interventions aimed at identifying and assisting victims, for donors who are developing and funding such protection programs. Protection projects include a wide range of interventions, from building the capacity of government and civil society stakeholders to the development and provision of services to victims, establishing appropriate legislation, regulations and policies. The following report highlights what we have learned from past and ongoing anti-trafficking interventions and research. Detailed information on how to develop programs based on these lessons learned is provided in the Tool Kit for Designing Trafficking Protection Programs (Annex B). A summary of the analysis of protection programs and the key recommendations is provided below and divided into the following categories:

A. Identification
B. Direct Assistance
C. Legal Proceedings as They Relate to Victims
D. Monitoring and Evaluation of Assistance Programs
E. Quantifying Trafficking
F. Trafficking Program Management and Design

The full analysis and complete recommendations follows in the main body of the report.

A. Identification

In the E&E region, many people believe that human trafficking is a violation of women for the purpose of prostitution. There is a lack of understanding of the other forms of trafficking and the wide range of people who can become victims. As a result, victims who do not conform to the 'expected' victim are often not identified as victims of trafficking. We tend to find what we look for, and anti-trafficking stakeholders in this region have been well trained to be on the lookout for the trafficking of young women for prostitution. As a result, these are the victims they have found. In areas where efforts have been made to demonstrate the trafficking of other groups, such as men for labor, more such victims have begun to be identified. Efforts need to be made to continue to improve and expand identification efforts, raising awareness amongst anti-trafficking actors that victims of trafficking can include men, women and children, of all ages, nationalities and ethnicities, trafficked for a wide range of exploitative purposes.

Improved identification and referral for assistance amongst key stakeholders such as law enforcement, border officials, consular officers and others should be addressed not only by providing training, but also through the development and implementation of clear operational procedures. These procedures help ensure that the theory learned in training is implemented appropriately and effectively, and is sustained long after the training is completed. Training should be incorporated into existing pre- and in-service training mechanisms in the country in order to ensure sustainability.

Hotlines combined with targeted awareness-raising campaigns are excellent ways of increasing reporting of cases. Such efforts in the region have resulted in increases in cases of self reporting, referrals from family or friends, and even reporting by clients. Development of hotlines and awareness-raising campaigns to increase the use of hotlines for reporting cases of trafficking and identification of victims should be encouraged. Care should be taken to fund awareness-raising campaigns with which victims and their families will identify, avoiding violent or provocative imagery and the use of off-putting terms such as victim, trafficking, and prostitution.

B. Assistance

As noted above, victims who do not conform to the expected demographic are often not identified as trafficked. Additionally, once identified these victims of trafficking may be offered very limited assistance, as assistance frameworks are generally designed for women trafficked into prostitution. Assistance programs need to be expanded to include all potential victim populations – men, women and children, trafficked for prostitution, labor, begging, etc.

Most of the countries in the region have national referral mechanisms in place – whether formal or informal. There are concerns, however that the implementation of these mechanisms is not always made in the best interest of the victims, but that political issues can take precedence. Victims may not be identified and assisted if States wish to reduce the numbers of victims identified. Similarly, victims' participation in such programs may not be voluntary if States wish to keep foreign victims in custody or wish to increase numbers assisted in order to increase funding for particular programs. Therefore, efforts should be made to ensure that referral mechanisms prioritize victims and are based on voluntary and informed participation. This can be ensured by designing referral mechanisms so that no one stakeholder has control and putting functioning monitoring mechanisms in place.

In order to increase identification and ensure informed participation in programs, informational materials for victims of trafficking are needed. In countries of origin, materials should be developed for distribution to potential victims of trafficking prior to their departure from the country, informing them of assistance available in key destination countries and providing contact details abroad and at home. Research has shown that some victims have avenues for escape. However, they may be reluctant to use them if they do not know where to turn to for help once freed. Therefore, providing information to potential victims, especially migrants, about where to turn for help is critical.

Many victims of trafficking return home who have not been identified as trafficked. They may return on their own or be deported for immigration violations (Dettmeijer-Vermeulen, Boot-Matthijssen, van Dijk, de Jonge van Ellemeet, Koster, & Smit ,2008, pp. 55-57; Kiryan & van der Linden, 2005, p. 37; IOM, 2007a, p. 2; IOM, 2006c, p. 3; Stephens & van der Linden, 2005, p. 30; Surtees, 2005, p. 17). To increase identification and assistance for this population, materials should also be developed which inform potential victims of trafficking on their return home of their rights and of the assistance available to them, by all assistance providers in the country. This should be made available to all returning migrants – but especially those deported, returning without documents, or returning under other unusual circumstances.

Many reports point to the large numbers of victims of trafficking who were freed from their trafficking situation by authorities in the destination country only to be deported as an irregular migrant, never being identified as trafficked. Many victims do not wish to be identified as trafficked and may be fearful of admitting what happened to them. However, providing information in writing which informs potential victims of trafficking upon identification of their rights and of the assistance options available to them could help increase their self-identification. Countries of destination should develop such materials which should be made available in the main languages spoken by VOTs and migrants in the country.

Violations of victims' rights do not end with their trafficking. Many continue to have their rights violated by those tasked with assisting them. Donors should encourage the development of monitoring mechanisms to ensure that victims' rights are not violated in the provision of services and that victims' rights take precedence over those of the State or law enforcement.

Currently most of the assistance programs were developed with donor funding and continue to operate with foreign assistance. However, there are numerous examples of cost sharing throughout the region which could be replicated elsewhere. In the development and funding of new programs, donors should encourage cost-sharing mechanisms with the state or local government. Other cost sharing mechanisms can also be developed, but care should be taken to ensure that such mechanisms (as well as cost-cutting measures) do not negatively impact on services or cause violations of the rights of victims.

Low income has been stated repeatedly as a push factor which increases vulnerability to the false promises of traffickers. Studies of migrants throughout this region show that most decide to migrate in order to earn a better income (Kiryan & van der Linden, 2005; Stephens & van der Linden, 2005; Ghinararu & van der Linden, 2004; Michailov, *et al.*, 2005; Winrock, 2004c). After their escape from trafficking, they are usually still in need of earning a living – either for themselves or to support their families. Assistance programs which do not address this need for income generation are not likely to succeed. Income generation activities for victims of trafficking should be encouraged, including employment programs, cooperative businesses and even entrepreneurship programs, when appropriate. Linkages to existing state and private mechanisms in the country should be developed so as to encourage sustainability: for example, through state employment offices or private micro-credit schemes.

As noted in the identification section above, monitoring is essential to ensure that the referral mechanisms are implemented as intended, that minimum standards of care are being utilized, and that the victim's rights are being respected. Complaint mechanisms, which are clear and easy to understand and use, should be incorporated into every program. Donors should support programs which develop sustainable monitoring mechanisms in the country.

C. Legal Proceedings Related to Victims

There are few incentives for victims to testify against their traffickers, and many disincentives including lengthy investigation and court procedures, threats from traffickers, and exposure to the public. In order to encourage victims to testify, these disincentives need to be reduced and the incentives increased. Therefore, there needs to be increased use of alternative methods of testifying, where they exist in law, to protect victims and lessen the burden on them of cooperating with justice. In places where such alternatives do not yet exist, donors could fund programs to reform the legislation to allow them, as well as to then encourage their use.

Other reforms which reduce the burden of testifying should also be developed. For example, legislation to protect victims' identity by making it illegal for media or others to release identifying information about victims to the public would go a long way in preventing victims' identities from being publicly exposed. Training and development of codes of ethics for journalists can also be encouraged. In countries where it is not yet the case, encourage reform of legislation to provide amnesty for crimes committed while trafficked.

In order to increase the incentives for victims to testify, mechanisms should be developed for victims to claim compensation from traffickers or to receive compensation from the State. Many States of the region have such mechanisms in place, but their use has been limited. Donors should support programs designed to encourage the implementation and use of these mechanisms to pay compensation in order to set a precedent for the future.

D. Monitoring and Evaluation of Assistance Programs

As noted in the introduction to the report, monitoring plans for most of the donor-funded programs have been limited to output oriented results and limited efforts have been made to measure the impact of protection programs. Donors should ensure that monitoring mechanisms are in place to measure program impact as well as to ensure that no harm is caused by donor-funded programs which are being improperly implemented (refer to Annex B: Tool Kit for Designing Trafficking Protection Programs for assistance in developing appropriate impact indicators.

E. Quantifying Trafficking

The ultimate objective of anti-trafficking efforts is to reduce the amount of trafficking and the number of people trafficked. Therefore analyzing the impact of such efforts necessarily requires that one is able to estimate the number of victims of trafficking. Research can also be used to contradict popular myths – myths that could lead to more people being trafficked because they believe these falsehoods and are unaware of the true dynamics of trafficking (Watson, 2005d, p.8). Research can also be used to influence government action especially if government has been unwilling to recognize the problem of trafficking and the research makes a compelling case that it is a significant problem.

Quantifying the number of victims of trafficking is fraught with difficulties. Even quantifying the number of victims who have been identified is difficult. A lack of data sharing between countries of origin and destination results in severe under-reporting of the number of identified trafficked persons from countries of origin. At the same time, measuring changes in the number of identified trafficked persons does not tell us anything about changes in the actual number of people trafficked or the impact of our programs because changes in the numbers of people identified can result from many things, including increases or reductions in efforts to identify victims.

Trying to measure the overall prevalence of trafficking provides a way of measuring changes in trafficking over time and tells us much more about the overall impact of anti-trafficking efforts in a country. While difficult, some interesting methodologies have recently been employed to this end. Further studies of prevalence should be supported.

F. Trafficking Program Management and Design

The design and management of anti-trafficking programs has an effect on their impact. Long-term projects (three to five years), rather than short-term projects, allow implementers to have a longer horizon and implement more sustainable programming. Similarly, spreading money and resources amongst too many stakeholders through multiple sub-grants causes a management burden and can result in reduced impact.

Some anti-trafficking efforts have combined the provision of services for vulnerable groups with those for former victims of trafficking when feasible. This has the possibility of reducing the stigma associated with trafficking by allowing trafficked persons to blend with other populations. This can be done by combining prevention and protection programs or by integrating trafficked persons as beneficiaries into non-trafficking programs – for example, by assisting trafficked persons to apply for micro-credit programs designed for the general population. It is important, however, that impact data be disaggregated to better assess the impact of the projects on victim protection and to help ascertain if programs need to be adapted in some way to be effective for trafficked persons.

II. Purpose and Methodology

The overall purpose of this chapter is to assist the USAID Europe and Eurasia (E&E) Bureau, as well as other donors and implementers, to improve the effectiveness and impact of programs designed to counter trafficking in persons (TIP), leading to a reduction of TIP and its consequences.

In 2004, USAID funded an assessment of anti-trafficking prevention programs in the E&E region (see Rosenberg, 2004, for the full report). In the four years that have passed since then there have been several new assessments conducted as well as other new programs and developments in the region. This chapter is designed to assess trafficking protection programs – programs designed to provide protection and assistance to victims of trafficking. It is intended to help USAID and other interested parties to determine the strengths and weaknesses of program approaches to date, ascertain which projects are replicable and where anti-TIP efforts can be integrated into other relevant programming. A companion report has been written to validate the findings and assumptions of the Rosenberg report on programming designed to prevent TIP and to update our knowledge base from lessons learned in the intervening years

Countries covered by this chapter include: Albania, Armenia, Azerbaijan, Belarus, Bosnia and Herzegovina,[1] Bulgaria, Croatia, Cyprus, Georgia, Kazakhstan, Kosovo, Kyrgyzstan, Macedonia, Moldova, Romania, Russia, Serbia, Montenegro, Tajikistan, Turkey, Turkmenistan, Ukraine, and Uzbekistan.

A. Analytical Framework

The report stems from a review of current literature produced by various USAID anti-TIP activities, and publicly accessible and relevant assessments and evaluations from anti-TIP programs funded by other donors (for a complete list, see Annex A, References). Additionally, the author draws on some of her own experiences in implementing anti-trafficking programs in countries of the region.

From this base, lessons were drawn about best practices in protection programming. The focus of the analysis is on programmatic strategy and design, from the perspective of a donor. Many important lessons can be learned from the available research about the difficulties in implementation –

especially as regards the rights and needs of victims in the victim assistance framework. These are not analyzed in detail in this chapter, as these are lessons for the implementing agencies. Rather the report focuses on the role of the donor and what donors can take from these findings.

B. Limitations

As this chapter is based on a literature review, the author is necessarily limited to the information available in writing, through publicly available reports as well as reports to the donor. The author was able to access very few monitoring frameworks for the anti-trafficking projects in the region. While the general objectives and goals of the projects are provided in the project documents, measurements of the impact of the projects were generally not provided or were not clear or specific enough to demonstrate program impact. This was especially true for protection programs for which indicators provided by implementing organizations were generally output oriented, specifying only numbers served by various services, and often including demographic data about victims served, but little information about the impact of the services provided on victims' post-trafficking lives.

Without clear objectives, indictors and targets, and data measuring these indicators and targets it is nearly impossible to assess the impact of programs from a literature review. In fact, USAID itself has stated that measuring the impact of the programs they fund has been difficult (USAID, 2006, p. 26). This finding is consistent with several anti-trafficking assessments conducted in the region (Pojman & Timoshenko, 2007, p. 27-28; Somach, n.d.), as well as with the U.S. Government's Government Accountability Office's assessment of trafficking in which it found that most U.S. Government anti-trafficking projects had not been evaluated or assessed for impact. Additionally it found that most had overly broad objectives, rarely linked activities to intended outcomes and did not have clear and measurable indicators and targets, making it very difficult to measure the impact of the interventions (GAO, 2006; & GAO, 2007).

III. BACKGROUND

A. Overview of Trafficking in the Region

Many reports and articles already exist which provide comprehensive overviews of human trafficking in the E&E region. Therefore, the information will not be repeated here. It is enough to provide a very brief overview by stating that countries which comprise the E&E region include countries of origin, transit and destination. Many countries are combinations of both origin and destination or even all three. Some began as primarily countries of destination or transit and are now known also or even primarily as countries of origin. Some were known as countries of origin and are now known also to be countries of destination. In the early days of anti-trafficking interventions, most information was known about trafficking for the purpose of prostitution. It is now known that the region also includes trafficking for labor and for begging and that its victims include men, women and children. The dynamics of trafficking are in constant flux. Anti-trafficking actors must be alert for new forms of trafficking and changing victim demographics in order to meet these changes with effective responses. Anti-trafficking programs need to be designed with the flexibility to allow program managers to adjust programs to meet these changing dynamics in a timely way. The report that follows will highlight some of these changing dynamics and what they mean for victim protection responses.

B. USAID's Response

Between 2001 and 2006, USAID supported anti-trafficking efforts in 70 countries worldwide, spending approximately US$109 million (GAO, 2007, p. 7, and USAID, 2006, p. 6). In 2005 alone, USAID spent US$7.9 million on anti-trafficking projects in 15 countries in Europe and Eurasia (USAID, 2006, p. 18). Annex B provides a full list of the anti-trafficking programs reviewed for this paper.

Even with such significant outlays of resources, little impact of the programs has been clearly demonstrated. In a USAID publication from 2006, every trafficking project funded by USAID in 2005, totaling US$21.34 million, is summarized. In this chapter, however, only one impact result from one project is reported. At the end of the report, the authors state that evaluating programs and measuring impact has been difficult, but that more emphasis will be put on this in future (USAID, 2006, pp. 6 & 26).

This chapter is one step in that direction, attempting to highlight best practices and to recommend future directions both for programming and for measuring impact of ongoing and future programs. For the purposes of this chapter, best practices were those interventions for which positive impact had been demonstrated. Also included as good or best practices were those interventions which used methodologies which make them sustainable for the long-term and interventions which incorporated adaptations which addressed shortcomings identified in earlier studies.

C. Protection and Why It Is Important

For the purposes of this chapter, protection refers to the anti-trafficking interventions done to protect and assist trafficked persons. This is distinct from prevention in that the assistance is directed at those who have already been trafficked. It encompasses the range of interventions done to improve or assist in a trafficked person's exit from trafficking, identification, emergency assistance, relocation/repatriation, integration/ reintegration, as well as assistance to victims before, during and after court proceedings.

Throughout the region, government funds are limited and the demands for these funds extensive – for infrastructure development, health care, pension schemes, education, economic growth, etc. Diversion of these scare resources to assist what is seen as a very small population of victims of human trafficking is often politically untenable. As a result, when international donors do not provide the support for victim services, there is a dearth of services available to victims of trafficking. Many victims manage without assistance or services, but others cannot and reports indicate that victims may end up homeless (Surtees, 2008b), re-trafficked, or continuing in exploitative conditions, including but not limited to prostitution, in an effort to survive. As USAID is one of the largest contributors to anti-trafficking programming in the region, it can be assumed therefore that without USAID funding for victim services, such services would not have existed. But the impact of this does not end with the victim. Not only would the victim be left to fend for him or herself, but the traffickers would remain at large as there would be few successful prosecutions without victims as witnesses and fewer victims would be likely to testify without some level of protection and support.

IV. ANALYSIS OF PROTECTION PROGRAMS

While there was a dearth of concrete indicators available which measured the impact of protection programs in the region (as noted in Limitations above), there was enough available information to come to the conclusion that without the efforts of the USAID-funded anti-trafficking programs in the region, it is likely that victims of trafficking would rarely be identified, their human rights would continue to be violated, and few would be willing to testify without support and protection. Similarly, our understanding of trafficking in the region would be severely limited. We have learned much over the years from the victims who have been assisted through donor-funded programs. Without this information we would still be laboring under misconceptions about trafficking, its victims and the perpetrators.

This chapter provides an analytical review of interventions aimed at identifying and assisting victims, for donors who are developing and funding such protection programs.[2] Protection projects include a wide range of interventions, from building the capacity of government and civil society stakeholders to the development and provision of services to victims, establishing appropriate legislation, regulations and policies. This chapter will highlight what we have learned from past and ongoing anti-trafficking interventions and research. Detailed information on how to develop programs based on these lessons learned is provided in the Tool Kit for Designing Trafficking Protection Programs (Annex B). The analysis of protection programs is divided into the following categories:

A. Identification
B. Direct Assistance
C. Legal Proceedings as they relate to Victims
D. Monitoring and Evaluation of Assistance Programs
E. Quantifying Trafficking
F. Trafficking Program Management and Design

A. Identification

Identification of victims of trafficking is critical. Most reports point to the hidden nature of trafficking and the fact that the number of victims identified and assisted represents just a small fraction of the population of actual victims.

In addition to those who never come to the attention of any authorities, there are many reports of victims being held in prisons and/or deported as irregular migrants having never been identified as victims of trafficking (Dettmeijer-Vermeulen, Boot-Matthijssen, van Dijk, de Jonge van Ellemeet, Koster, & Smit ,2008, pp. 55-57; Kiryan & van der Linden, 2005, p. 37; IOM, 2007a, p. 2; IOM, 2006c, p. 3; Stephens & van der Linden, 2005, p. 30; Surtees, 2005, p. 17).

Failure to properly identify victims of trafficking is not only problematic in that we fail to assist those who may need it and to prosecute those who have broken the law, but also because it can impact our understanding of the trafficking dynamics in the country or region. For example, if we fail to identify local women in prostitution who are victims of trafficking we may assume that there is no domestic trafficking and therefore not make efforts to look for and address the issue. The same is true if we assume that all trafficking is for prostitution; we risk ignoring trafficking for labor or the needs of male victims of trafficking.

1. Problems of Identification

Definitions and Understanding of Trafficking

Does language or culture influence our understanding of trafficking and our ability to therefore identify victims of trafficking? In many countries of the region, terms related to trafficking are defined through the local language which does not always have an exact equivalent, such as ‘contraband’ for smuggling (Kelly, 2005, p. 36) or ‘trade’ or ‘sale’ for trafficking. If one translates trafficking as the sale of a person, this may make it necessary to prove the actual sale and purchase of the individual to prove trafficking, a requirement far beyond any expressed in the UN Protocol.

Studies of trafficking in the region have found that even anti-trafficking actors, those whom one would expect to have the clearest understanding of trafficking, demonstrated widespread misconceptions and misunderstandings. Some may stem from these linguistic confusions. In other cases anti-trafficking actors seemed to be searching for definitions that provided for ‘deserving’ or ‘innocent’ victims, which lead again to a much narrower definition of trafficking and therefore the possibility that actual victims of trafficking as defined by the UN Protocol could go unidentified and unassisted (Kelly, 2005, pp. 37-38; Brunovskis & Surtees, 2005, p. 46; Bjerkan & Dyrlid, 2005, pp. 143-144). Similar attitudes might impact on ethnic minorities or others for whom the exploitation as defined by the UN Protocol is considered as 'typical' of their culture and therefore not really trafficking and not requiring intervention or assistance (Bjerkan & Dyrlid, 2005, p. 145).

Victims May Not Wish To Be Identified As Trafficked

Many people, whose experiences would qualify them as victims of trafficking under the UN Protocol definition, prefer not to be identified as such. There are a myriad of reasons for this – shame at the term trafficking and its association with prostitution, the implication of failure that the term victim implies, fear of the trafficker and not wanting to report him or her, a lack of recognition that what happened to them was a violation of their rights and a crime against them, even a desire to move on and continue in search of the life they had been in pursuit of (GAATW, 2007, preface; Brunovskis & Surtees 2005; Bjerkan & Dyrlid, 2005, p. 149-150).

Some awareness-raising programs have attempted to address this by reducing the public shame and stigma attached to trafficking (IOM 2005g; IOM 2006b). Additionally, programs to support and protect victims of trafficking need to be designed in such a way as to promote the beneficiaries' aspirations rather than their needs as perceived by service providers or the needs of law enforcement or other anti-trafficking actors..

We Find What We Look For - Neglected Victim Populations

Until recently, there has been a general assumption that victims of trafficking tend to be women and children, trafficked mainly for the purpose of prostitution. This is especially so in the Europe and Eurasia region, where interventions have tended to focus on this one form of trafficking. Authorities were trained to be on the lookout for such cases, and, as a result, they began to find more and more of them, thereby confirming the assumptions. There is a tendency among anti-trafficking actors to recognize only victims who conform to a specific expected population of trafficking victim or as defined through operational procedures. As a result, there may be significant trafficking of other populations which is never recognized – such as for national women in prostitution, women trafficked for purposes other than prostitution, men trafficked for labor, prostitution and other purposes, and children trafficked for a variety of purposes.

In Bosnia, for example, many law enforcement actors believe that police are more inclined to identify foreign women in prostitution as victims of trafficking and refer them on for assistance through the established channels, than local women in prostitution. As a result, local women and girls in prostitution are not interviewed to determine if they are victims of trafficking and are not referred for assistance (Rosenberg, 2006, p. 14). This is a finding confirmed in other research in the region (c.f. Brunovskis & Surtees, 2007; Matei, 2005).

Similarly, in Central Asia there was an assumption that there were more female victims of trafficking for sexual exploitation than for other purposes. This has proven not to be true, with studies showing that there are far more victims of trafficking for labor than for sexual exploitation, including both male and female victims (Kelly, 2005, p. 39). Many other studies document that male victims of trafficking may be less likely to be identified for the same reasons (Dottridge, 2007, p. 17; Michailov, van der Linden, & Scanlan, 2005, p. 45; c.f. Surtees, 2008a and Surtees, 2008b), including examples of male victims of trafficking who fail to be identified even after extensive contact with authorities (Surtees, 2007b, pp. 77-83; Surtees, 2008b).

However, as there has been an increase in awareness of trafficking for labor and of trafficking for men, more such cases are now being confirmed. In countries where more attention has recently been paid to the issue, there have been increasing numbers of male victims of trafficking identified, as can be seen in the table below.

Street children may also be a neglected population, where they are not recognized as victims of trafficking or as a group vulnerable to trafficking. A recent survey in Albania revealed widespread sexual exploitation of street children (Terre des Hommes, 2008). Many countries of the region have significant numbers of children begging on the streets (Fritz, 2006, p. 6; Limanowska, 2007, 61; Surtees, 2005, p. 38; DOS, 2007). While it is not known how many of these children may be victims of trafficking, the Albanian study indicates that street children may be at a higher risk of trafficking. There are, however, very few protection and assistance programs in the region for street children who may be trafficked for begging or sexual exploitation. This highlights the need to increase efforts to identify and assist this potentially vulnerable group.

The same is likely to be true of other forms of trafficking. This highlights the importance of improving identification mechanisms for all demographics, and raising awareness amongst anti-trafficking actors that people of all ages, nationalities, ethnicities and genders are trafficked for a wide range of exploitative purposes. Improving and expanding identification efforts should be a critical component of protection programs.

Table 1. Identified Male Victims of Trafficking from Belarus and Ukraine

Country	2004		2005		2006	
	Number	Percent	Number	Percent	Number	Percent
Belarus	28	11.3	157	28.4	159	38.4
Ukraine	68	17.2	113	16.1	160	19
Romania			557	21.8	542	23.7

Sources: Surtees, 2008a, p. 8 and ICMPD, 2007, Annex: Country Report Romania

2. Identification through Law Enforcement Channels

Identification in many countries is done primarily by law enforcement officials (Dettmeijer-Vermeulen *et al.,* 2008, p. 50; IOM, 2006a, p. 6; IOM, 2007a, p. 2; Rosenberg, 2006, p. 14). Clearly therefore, interventions aimed at raising the awareness and capacity of law enforcers to identify victims of trafficking are necessary. However, there are also reports that frequent turnover and rotation of law enforcement officers and border guards reduces the impact of such training over time. In Albania the number of referrals for assistance of irregular female migrants identified at the border declined from 24 percent in 2006 to less than one percent in 2007, even as the number of identified irregular migrants increased dramatically - from 99 to 293 (Creative Associates International, Inc., 2007b, p. 3). While there may be many explanations for this phenomenon, one possible reason expounded by stakeholders in Albania[3] is that the border guards who were trained on trafficking and worked on the issue for many years have been transferred to other positions.

This illustrates that training by itself is not sufficient to maintaining long-term impact; it is important to build internal procedures requiring law enforcement to refer victims for assistance. It is believed in Bosnia that law enforcers are better at identifying and referring foreign victims of trafficking because of the training they have received as well as the procedures that are in place when a foreign woman in prostitution is identified (Rosenberg, 2006, p. 14). Such procedures should be in place throughout the region, and should be expanded to include identification of other categories of victims of trafficking – male and female, adults and minors, trafficked for any form of exploitation.

It is important to note that some reports indicate that law enforcers do not always refer victims or presumed victims for assistance regardless of how well they are trained (Snajdrova & Hancilova, 2007, p. 25; Iselin, 2007;

Limanowska, 2007). The reasons for this may vary from country to country or even from officer to officer. Clearly, research into the reasons why officers may fail to refer victims would be helpful in finding ways to address the phenomenon. It is therefore important that other avenues of victim identification are also strengthened, as described below.

Good Practice: Improved Identification by Law Enforcers

Combine training with clear operational procedures to improve identification of victims of trafficking of all ages, nationalities, ethnicities and genders, trafficked for a wide range of exploitative purposes.

3. Identification through Other Key Stakeholders

In addition to law enforcers, other key actors can play a critical role in the identification of victims of trafficking, especially consular officials, medical personnel (especially those at clinics frequented by migrant workers or sex workers), immigration officials, and others. Interviews with trafficked and exploited migrants has shown that migrants believe that their consulates abroad could be useful sources of information and support (Ghinararu & van der Linden, 2004, p. 41; Michailov *et al.*, 2005, p. 47; Kiryan & van der Linden, 2005, p. 40). In some reports, training for consular officials has been associated with increases in the identification of VOTs by consular officials and more efficient processing of cases. In Uzbekistan, they reported a reduction from two months to two weeks to repatriate a victim of trafficking after consular training (Watson, 2005d, pp. 9-10). Many countries of Southeastern Europe (SEE) have also shown a positive trend toward identification of VOTs by consular officials and others, such as social workers, doctors, family and friends, after training and outreach (Surtees, 2005, p. 44).

In Bulgaria, not only have consular officials and embassy staff been trained to identify VOTs, but the Ministry of Foreign Affairs has also developed mandatory referral mechanisms for such cases (Surtees, 2005, p. 203). In Kazakhstan, instructions were also sent out to all consular missions abroad about how to provide assistance to victims of trafficking (Kelly, 2005, p. 78). While the impact of this could not be assessed because recent statistics on the number of identifications by consular officials could not be obtained for this chapter, it would appear to be a useful combination of tactics – combining training with formalized operational procedures.

Much training for a wide variety of professionals has been undertaken throughout the region. One study in Serbia noted however, that there were vast differences between the amount of training received by types of professionals and by location. For example, police officers received far more training than prosecutors and judges, and all professionals in the capital received far more training than those residing elsewhere (Simeunovic-Patic, 2005, p. 23). Nonetheless, improvements in identification by anti-trafficking actors became more pro-active. Some of this improvement is arguably attributable to the capacity building efforts, but as well, it is important to note that there was high level government support (Simeunovic-Patic, 2005, p. 49-50).

GOOD PRACTICE: SUSTAINABLE TRAINING

Integration of training into existing pre- and in-service training mechanisms, and combining such training with clear operational procedures, makes for a sustainable approach to improved victim identification and referral for assistance. This is especially true for key target groups, such as law enforcers, consular officials, immigration authorities, medical practitioners and social workers.

4. Identification through Awareness-Raising and Hotlines

In many countries, hotlines, in combination with awareness-raising campaigns, often set up for prevention purposes, have been instrumental in identifying, rescuing and referring victims for assistance (IOM, 2003, p. 14; Watson, 2005b-d; Kelly, 2005, p. 89). For example, in Kazakhstan, nine calls to the hotline in a three-month period (Jan-Mar 2005) were about specific cases of trafficking. During that same period in Uzbekistan, 333 calls came about specific cases of trafficking (IOM, 2005e). In 2003 in Tajikistan, two percent of calls were specifically about trafficking cases, nine of which were calls about missing persons, and of these, five resulted in the successful identification of the missing person (Kelly, 2005, p. 89). In Bulgaria, two hotlines combined received 128 calls in 2003 and 103 in 2004 that were either reports of missing persons/suspected VOTs or calls from VOTs themselves (Surtees, 2005, p. 203). In Macedonia, during the first three years of operation, 10.5 percent of calls to the hotline were related to missing persons or actual victims of trafficking (Stefkovska-Veljanovska, 2005, p. 17). In Turkey, 109 victims were identified and assisted from calls to the hotline (IOM 2006e).

It should be noted that calls to national hotlines are made both from within and outside the country. Victims may contact their national hotlines after being trafficked abroad. Hotlines should have numbers which can be dialed from abroad (or dual numbers – a local emergency number, short and easy to remember, and a regular number which can be dialed from abroad).[4]

Hotlines alone do not appear to be sufficient for increasing identification, however. Hotlines need to be accompanied by awareness-raising campaigns so that the public is aware of the existence of the hotline. Campaigns can be targeted to improve their effectiveness as an identification tool. Stigma associated with trafficking, as well as a lack of familiarity with the term trafficking (ASA, 2005, p.11), means that awareness-raising campaigns should consider using other terminology with which presumed victims or the public might be more familiar and with which they may be more likely to associate themselves. Similarly, in many cases, the imagery used in awareness-raising campaigns has been found to be too severe, so that victims of trafficking do not identify with it and therefore do not identify as victims of trafficking (Rosenberg, 2004, p. 15) or do not believe that their situation was severe enough to warrant assistance (Brunovskis & Surtees, 2007, p. 137). To be effective identification tools, campaigns should be designed not for provocation or to instill fear, but to reflect the complex reality of trafficking and exploitation in such a way that victims and their families recognize their own situation in them.

GOOD PRACTICE: HOTLINES

Market hotlines to increase identification of victims. Avoid imagery and terminology which can alienate the target group – provocative or violent images and terms like victim, trafficking, prostitution.

Targeting clients of prostitution in awareness-raising campaigns can also be an important route toward increasing identification. Clients have been shown to be an important avenue of rescue for victims of trafficking. In Bosnia, where there was a targeted awareness-raising campaign towards users of prostitution, a large number of victims of trafficking for prostitution have been identified and referred for assistance by clients. In 2003, 13 percent of foreign VOTs were identified by clients. In 2004, this rose to 18 percent of foreign VOTs and five percent of national VOTs (Surtees, 2005, p. 152). However, there have been few such programs designed to reach out to potential clients. A study of men in Kosovo who had used the services of a prostitute within the preceding 12 months found that although most were fairly well informed about trafficking, most knew of no organizations providing assistance to victims (Prism, 2007, p. 67). And while they expressed sympathy for the victims, they expressed a fear of reporting cases to authorities and a belief that authorities would not take any action (Prism, 2007, p. 68).

Good Practice: Government Run Hotlines

In Albania, the government launched a helpline with support of international donors. Donors provided equipment, training and support for the development of a handbook for operators. The government provides the space as well as frontline operators for 24/7 coverage. Operators divert calls to the police trafficking unit, an anti-trafficking IO, and a health-related organization, depending on the nature of the call.

Do No Harm

Donors should be careful when selecting organizations to implement hotlines. It is critical that hotlines are staffed by properly trained professionals and that these professionals have clear guidelines for how to handle calls. They are taking calls that can result in harm to themselves and others if not handled properly. In cases of rescue, there are particularly high security threats, where the lives of the victim, those around them and those assisting them can be endangered if not handled professionally. Unexpected harm can result even from calls intended to prevent trafficking. For example, two VOTs in Kyrgyzstan had contacted a hotline about work abroad. They were assured by the authorities to whom they were referred that the company had a license for organizing employment abroad and they were also given what appeared to be legitimate work contracts. While the information about the company's license was correct, it gave the women a false sense of security and they found themselves trafficked nonetheless (Winrock 2004a: 31 and 32). There have also been cases of hotline operators being threatened by traffickers so that it is important that hotlines implement policies to protect the employees (Watson 2005d: 10).

This concern points to the important role which hotlines can play to allow for anonymous reporting, especially if they are properly marketed to this target group. In places where hotlines are already in place, marketing specifically to clients should not entail a significant increase in costs as the same hotline can be used, it is only necessary to target the awareness-raising message appropriately.

It was noted that in many countries there seemed to be a multitude of competing hotlines (Watson, 2005b, p. 24; Pojman & Timoshenko, 2007, p. 4; Iselin (2007). While there may be no harm in having multiple hotlines, it is also not clear that there is any advantage, so long as one hotline is accessible throughout the country and can be accessed from abroad. Clearly, for donors with increasingly limited budgets it is foolish to fund multiple hotlines when one will do. When donor funding ends, multiple hotlines will be harder to sustain than one.

5. Identification through Bilateral Relationships

As noted earlier, in many countries of destination, victims of trafficking are not identified as such when they come to the attention of authorities. In many cases they are incarcerated or deported as irregular migrants or for crimes committed while trafficked. In some cases, relationships between origin and destination countries – both between authorities and also between NGOs, can be effective in improving the identification process and referring the identified victims of trafficking for assistance. For example, in Uzbekistan, relationships between a local Uzbek NGO and NGOs in Israel and Thailand have resulted in the identification and rescue of Uzbek victims of trafficking being held in prison on prostitution or immigration charges (Kelly, 2005, p. 86).

Study visits to destination countries have also resulted in identification of victims. Officials from both Tajikistan and Uzbekistan went to the United Arab Emirates on study visits. As a result of these trips bilateral discussions on trafficking were held for the first time and 18 Tajik and over 30 Uzbek victims of trafficking were voluntarily repatriated (IOM, 2005c, pp. 10, 12). It is not clear from the reports how the victims were identified and located – seemingly by Tajik and Uzbek officials interviewing their citizens held in UAE prisons. It is also not clear if the established bilateral relationship continued to result in victim identification and repatriation or if the identification and repatriation stopped once the working visit ended.

Given the cost of study visits, the author only recommends such an approach in cases where one country denies the existence of victims of trafficking from the other. In such cases, a visiting delegation from the country of origin could undertake an assessment mission to meet with their citizens directly as well as to negotiate with the destination country. The results of such an assessment can be used to change attitudes and negotiate for lasting changes.

However, other opportunities for multi-purpose visits should be used to encourage victim identification and referral mechanisms. When groups are going for study trips or to attend workshops or conferences, it would be useful to add on time to examine the issue.

B. Direct Assistance

Much of the direct support for victims of trafficking in this region has historically been funded by international donors and provided by local NGOs. Without international donor support, most victims in this region would not have received the necessary assistance.

It is important for donors to understand their role in ensuring that those to whom they provide the funding have the necessary skills and experience to provide such assistance. Much harm can be inflicted unintentionally. Victims can be unnecessarily traumatized, may be at risk for suicide and are often threatened or even murdered by their traffickers. Those supporting victims are also at risk, as well as victims' family and loved ones. Similarly, those working alongside trafficked persons can be at risk during rescue operations. It is critical, therefore, that victim assistance be undertaken only by those with the appropriate experience, and donors have a responsibility to ensure that they do not give money for such assistance to organizations which do not have the skills and experience to handle it properly.

DO NO HARM

Unintended harm can be inflicted when providing direct assistance to vulnerable persons, in spite of the best of intentions. Donors have a responsibility to ensure that the organizations they fund have the necessary skills and experience to undertake the task.

This section will highlight issues for donors to take into consideration when designing and managing projects which provide support for direct assistance to victims of trafficking.

1. Neglected Victim Populations

As noted in Section A, Identification, most of the assistance programs in the region have been designed specifically for adult female victims of trafficking, often specifically for victims of trafficking for sexual exploitation. Much of our statistics and other information about trafficking come from studying the group of assisted victims, therefore there has been an assumption that most victims are women trafficked for forced prostitution.

We have made other assumptions as well, for example, that women from families with a history of domestic violence are more vulnerable to trafficking, which is addressed in a recent USAID study entitled *Examining the Intersection between Trafficking in Persons and Domestic Violence* (Warnath, 2007). The study found that there is ample anecdotal evidence linking trafficking and domestic violence, but statistics on relation between the two are too sparse to be representative. While it is true that a large portion of the assisted population in many countries in this region come from abusive homes (Surtees, 2005; MNAdvocates 2000), it is possible that this abuse did not make them any more susceptible to the traffickers, but rather, that those with strong family ties, while equally at risk for trafficking, do not seek assistance as they have enough support from within their family circle and therefore do not show up in statistics about victims (Brunovskis & Surtees, 2007, p. 66). There may be many other such assumptions that are made based on the assisted victim population that impact on the assistance we provide.

As we have learned more about trafficking in the region, it has become clear that there are other victim populations who are not included in our data on trafficking because they have not yet received assistance, but who may nevertheless be in need of services. These include children, children of victims of trafficking, victims of trafficking for purposes other than prostitution, male victims of trafficking and victims of trafficking with mental or physical disabilities. Assistance may not currently be structured in such a way as to be accessible or useful for these populations.

If we do not correct this, we may create a vicious cycle whereby we continue to support our misconceptions about victims by the way in which we provide assistance, and therefore continue to ignore the needs of populations which do not fit within our framework. Donors should design programs in such a way that they are flexible enough to identify and address the needs of victims of all ages, gender, and ethnicities, and do not conform to our current stereotypes. Donors should support the development of assistance programs specifically designed for the needs of these target groups; children, for example, should not simply be incorporated into assistance programs designed for adults, just as men should not be integrated into programs designed for women. Each group has special needs which must be addressed.

2. Coordination and Referral Networks

Collaboration with a multitude of stakeholders is important for assuring that victims receive the range of services necessary for their recovery. In many cases it is not the organizations which provide direct assistance to victims who are the first to come into contact with them, but rather this is often the police or border guards or Embassy officials. They need to know to whom they can refer victims for necessary assistance. Similarly, not all assisting organizations can provide the full range of assistance needed by victims. Therefore they need to refer to and collaborate with one another in order to ensure that all of the victims' needs are met. Therefore, referral networks are an important part of the victim assistance framework.

National Referral Mechanisms

Most of the countries in this region have existing national referral mechanisms. The OSCE & ODIHR (2004) define the national referral mechanism as:

> a co-operative framework through which state actors fulfil their obligations to protect and promote the human rights of trafficked persons, co-ordinating their efforts in a strategic partnership with civil society. The basic aims of an NRM are to ensure that the human rights of trafficked persons are respected and to provide an effective way to refer victims of trafficking for services. In addition, NRMs can work to help improve national policy and procedures on a broad range of victim-related issues such as residence and repatriation regulations, victim compensation, and witness protection. NRMs can establish national plans of action and can set benchmarks to assess whether goals are being met (p.15).

A properly functioning referral mechanism should provide the best possible and widest range of assistance for victims of trafficking. However, typically, there are some problems in implementation including: 1) conditionality, which may result from who controls the system, and 2) competition amongst service providers. Both are discussed below.

Conditionality

There are reports from the region of victim assistance, or at least some aspects of assistance, being conditional upon agreeing to cooperate with law enforcement and/or law enforcement being able to control who is referred for assistance (Limanowska, 2007, p. 74-75; ICMPD, 2007, Annex: Country Report Romania; DOS, 2007, p. 63). This is especially concerning as this trend could increase as governments assume more responsibility for and financing of assistance. It is conceivable that they may increase conditionality in order to restrict services and contain costs. It may also be politically difficult to justify the provision of extensive services to victims of trafficking when other vulnerable persons are also in need of assistance in the country. Restricting assistance to those willing to cooperate with justice may be more politically acceptable. Therefore, programs need to be designed in such a way as to reduce the likelihood of this happening. One method may be to ensure that victim identification and referral mechanisms include civil society actors and do not turn over all authority and responsibility to law enforcement. Monitoring of referral mechanisms is also critical to ensuring that victims' rights are respected, not only in the written procedures, but also in their implementation. (See sub-section B-10, "Standards, Regulations and Monitoring of Assistance" for more information on this point.)

Competition

Some USAID-funded programs dedicate a significant portion of funding to coordination and information sharing among anti-trafficking actors. For example, in Albania, one USAID-funded project has a specific component of its program dedicated to coordination, specifically 'to promote improved coordination of trafficking prevention activities and assistance programs for victims of trafficking between civil society and government, as well as among civil society actors…to improve the quality and efficiency of prevention programs and direct assistance to victims of trafficking [and] to enhance the geographic distribution of programs and services more evenly throughout the country' (CAII, 2006, p. 4). While a mid-term evaluation found that most of the participants felt that the coordination aspects of the project were useful (EnCompass, 2006), there has not yet been enough time to measure the ways in which improved coordination has led to improved assistance for victims, which would not have taken place without it. As well, there continue to be issues of competition amongst service providers in Albania which coordination does not seem to have eliminated (Surtees 2006). Many other countries face these issues of competition amongst service providers, perhaps a natural phenomenon when resources are scarce. Donors should be careful when designing programs so as not to encourage duplication of services and wasting valuable resources. They should also ensure that it is the victims of trafficking, the beneficiaries of the services, who are given the choice in service providers when competition exists (see sub-section B-3, "Informing Victims About Services", below, for some ideas on how donors can give beneficiaries the control over how and from whom they receive services).

Cross-Border Coordination / Repatriation

Currently, repatriation and cross-border coordination throughout the region tends to be handled by IOM with international donor funding. As funding declines, national governments will need to take over this function. Who will pay for repatriation, will it be voluntary, and will it be handled safely, effectively and with respect for the rights and dignity of the victims? These are critical considerations.

A project funded by USAID in ten countries of origin (most of them in SEE) is currently working to improve cross-border coordination via a formalized transnational referral mechanism. This project could play an important role in ensuring safe and respectful repatriation procedures are in place. However, it is too early to assess its impact and to extract lessons which could be applied more broadly throughout Europe and Eurasia.

3. Informing Victims about Services

Providing information to victims of trafficking and those at risk of being victimized (migrant workers, women in prostitution, etc.) is an important method of increasing identification and improving the provision of assistance to victims. In cases involving cross-border migration, information needs to be designed for distribution before potential victims depart from their country of origin, upon identification, before repatriation and also following repatriation.

Before Departure from Country of Origin

In countries of origin, there is a critical need to provide information to potential victims of trafficking about the assistance available to them in key destination countries as well as to make them aware of hotlines in their home country. Victims of trafficking may have more avenues for escape than they are sometimes given credit for having. A study in Ukraine found that even though victims of trafficking experienced significant violence, threats of violence and restrictions of their freedom of movement, many do retain some ability to escape. In fact 36 percent of those interviewed were able to escape either on their own or with help, compared to the 21 percent who exited via police raids (Kiryan & van der Linden, 2005, p. 38). A similar study in Albania found that over 30 percent were able to leave on their own or with help (Stephens & van der Linden, 2005, p. 30). A recent study of male victims of trafficking in Ukraine and Belarus found that three quarters of assisted Belarusian men and nearly half of assisted Ukrainian men escaped on their own (Surtees, 2008a, p. 57). Similarly in Georgia, a study found that just under half the victims of trafficking who were interviewed returned to Georgia on their own (IOM, 2001, p. 36).

After escaping, trafficked persons can face continued risks and hardship which could be avoided if assistance were provided. One study found examples of victims who, after escaping on their own, failed to receive assistance and walked hundreds of miles to get home, begged for food, were exploited by strangers they met along the way, and were interrogated and arrested at the border trying to reenter their country of residence (Surtees, 2007b). Several ILO studies in the region found that although victims of trafficking had pressing needs for assistance while in the destination country, they did not seek such assistance because the vast majority were unaware that assistance was available. Those who knew that assistance might be available tended not to request it either because they were unable to contact assistance providers or were afraid of being arrested and or deported (Kiryan & van der Linden, 2005, p. 38; Stephens & van der Linden, 2005, p. 31-32; Ghinararu & van der Linden, 2004, p. 38).

> As one victim stated: I knew nothing about the assistance available for trafficking victims. I didn't know whom to address in the destination country in case I needed help. I thought I could only go to the police. There I didn't have enough courage to go to the police because the [traffickers] used to say that they bought the police. They threatened me with death in case I went to the police. I was afraid (Surtees, 2007b, p. 95).

Given that so many people escape on their own, it is important that they have information about where they can turn for assistance when needed. A recent case in Mongolia illustrates the important link between the provision of information and escape from trafficking. In this case, several young women were separately trafficked to another Asian country. One had received a flyer on the train about trafficking which provided a hotline number in Mongolia. When the women realized they were never going to be able to escape on their own, one of them used a client's phone to make a call to the hotline in

Mongolia. They exchanged email addresses and continued communication through email whenever the women had access through a client until a rescue could be organized. The women are now safely back home.5 The efficacy of this mechanism is confirmed by other studies which show that victims often call hotlines in their own country while they are residing in a foreign country (Surtees, 2008a, p. 59).

After Identification and Before Repatriation

In countries of destination, it is important to provide victims with information about assistance upon identification, in a language which the victim understands. Studies of victims indicate that they frequently have no experience with assistance mechanisms or are not even aware that such things exist (Surtees, 2007b). They may be fearful and distrustful. They may need time to understand what is happening to them and what is being offered to them. Providing information upon identification in writing gives victims more time to absorb and understand the information.

Studies have shown that uncertainty is a critical factor which raises fear and anxiety in victims of trafficking and that transition phases, such as at identification and repatriation, were found to be those fraught with the most uncertainty. Researchers suggest that everything possible should be done to 'replace uncertainty with structure and predictability' (Bjerkan & Dyrlid, 2005, p. 125). From Bjerkan & Dyrlid, 2005:

> The NGO presented her with a list of services that was available to her while she was waiting for repatriation, and she also received information about what services would be available to her after her return to Moldova. Kacusa said it was important for her to receive this kind of information and that it made her feel more confident (p. 137).

GOOD PRACTICE: INFORMING VICTIMS

Because language barriers can lead to misunderstandings and law enforcers and assistance providers do not always have interpreters available, police in one European country are using iPods to assist in communicating with victims during raids and investigations. The iPods are preloaded with information about assistance in several languages (UN GIFT Conference, Vienna 2008).

A finding from several studies is that NGOs providing assistance in destination countries do not always know about the assistance that is available in countries of origin, to which those whom they are assisting will return. If they had more information about these programs, they could provide better information to victims about what to expect when they return home. Several studies have recommended study tours and other methods of increasing communication between colleagues in countries of origin and destination (Rosenberg, 2006; Bjerkan & Dyrlid, 2005). Simple, low cost methods should also be employed whenever possible. Email or even Voice Over Internet Protocol communication (i.e., Skype) between the victim and service providers in the country to which they will be returning is an effective way to initiate contact, to lessen anxiety and to ensure continuity of services for the victim.

Upon Return to Country of Origin

Many victims of trafficking come to the attention of authorities as irregular migrants and are never identified as victims of trafficking. In the Ukrainian study referred to on the previous page, of the 21 percent of interviewed victims of trafficking who were freed during police raids, only six percent were identified as victims of trafficking and referred for assistance. The rest were arrested and deported (Kiryan & van der Linden, 2005). In the Albanian study, approximately 50 percent of the victims of trafficking they interviewed exited via police raid and of these only 5.6 percent were referred for assistance. The others were arrested and deported (Stephens & van der Linden, 2005, p. 30).

Good Practice: Giving Victims Choice among Service Providers

The U.S. Government provides an example of good practice in this regard, providing all certified victims of trafficking with a list of organizations providing assistance throughout the United States, giving the victim the choice of where and from whom to receive services (DOJ 2007: 2).

Given the number of victims of trafficking who are deported without being identified it is critical to set up mechanisms for identifying victims upon repatriation and providing them with information about assistance. Many will not admit details of their experience when they are interviewed at the border by police. However, alternative methods can be used. Information about assistance can be provided in writing so that victims can contact service providers at a later date. As well, some countries are experimenting with having social workers present at the border during interviews to see if this improves identification.[6] While the impact of such interventions is not yet known, expanding methodologies to increase identification is critical.

Competition

Competition amongst service providers can also lead to victims not receiving the full range of services available to them (Brunovskis & Surtees 2007: 79). In most countries victims are not given choices about the range of assistance and assistance providers available to them. They are, rather, referred to one organization and not informed about alternatives.

Donors have an opportunity to take the lead on providing full and open information to victims of trafficking by ensuring that the informational materials they fund use language which does not alienate potential victims (by focusing on exploitation and migration, perhaps, rather than trafficking, victimization or prostitution; by ensuring that the information is distributed in ways to expand its reach; and by ensuring that the information provided includes the widest range of assistance available and not the assistance of only one service provider).

4. Shelters

Most of the shelters for victims of trafficking operating in the E&E region were established by and continue to operate with international donor funding. In places where such funding has not been forthcoming there is often a reported lack of shelters available, as in Russia, for example (Tiurukanova, 2006). Sadly, in many countries of this region, where many donors have provided funding for anti-trafficking efforts, there is sometimes a reported excess of shelter capacity, competition between shelter providers, and shelters lying empty (Rosenberg, 2006; Watson, 2005b, p. 16; USAID, 2007, p.8).

Shelters are a critical part of a comprehensive package of services for victims of trafficking. Long-term accommodation or shelter provides a necessary component to victim recovery – a safe, affordable place to live – especially for victims without family support. Most long-term shelters are located in places where victims are able to find employment or attend vocational training while receiving services (USAID, 2007, p. 9). Temporary shelter can also be important during different phases of post trafficking life, for example, prior to repatriation and just before returning to one's family or establishing an independent life. But there could also be other times when shelter is needed – for example, during the trial if the trial is taking place in a city other than where the victim is currently a resident (Winrock, 2004a, p. 34).

Therefore it is critical to provide shelter services in a flexible way, which can meet the needs of victims while being cost effective and sustainable. Much has been written about shelters, about the positive and negative aspects of services provided in shelters, about their rules and regulations, and about services provided within them. It is not possible in this chapter to go into such detail. The author recommends that service providers refer to the many useful guidebooks and research reports on the subject. A few of the many that are available include:

- *The IOM Handbook on Direct Assistance for Victims of Trafficking* (IOM, 2007d),
- Anti-Slavery International's *Protocol for Identification and Assistance to Trafficked Persons and Training Kit* (2005),
- UNICEF's *Guidelines for the Protection of Child Victims of Trafficking* (2006),
- ILO's *Psycho-Social Rehabilitation of Children Withdrawn from Trafficking and Other Worst Forms of Child Labour* (2007), and
- *Listening to Victims*, by Rebecca Surtees (2007).

Donors should be familiar with some of the problems noted in these reports and should ensure that monitoring systems are in place to prevent violations of victims' rights occurring within the assistance framework (see sub-section B-10, "Standards, Regulations and Monitoring of Assistance" for more on this point).

5. Sustainability of Services

Providing services for victims of trafficking is costly, and shelter services are arguably the single most expensive aspect of victim services. With declining donor funding, service providers need to both lower costs and find creative local ways to fund services.

Lowering Costs

In some countries, as the number of identified victims in need of shelter services has declined dramatically (usually due to reductions in the number of identified victims[7]), there is an excess of shelter capacity, with beautiful, costly shelters lying empty more often than not (Rosenberg, 2006). Given the vast need for a wide variety of social services throughout the region, this is a shocking waste of resources, and makes shelter services that much less sustainable over the long run. Closing shelters, remobilizing them for other populations, or finding other ways to reduce costs is critical.

Care must be taken, however when cutting costs so that services do not suffer as a result. Often staff is the first resource to be cut, and yet they are the most critical asset of any shelter. Overburdened staff are not effective. Not only can this result in emotional burn-out of the staff and neglect of the residents, but it could also result in poor decision-making, putting victims and staff at risk. Bjerkan & Dyrlid (2004) provide an example of an overburdened staff member who was on duty alone at night when one resident fell ill at the same time as a new resident, who had been physically assaulted, arrived and the remaining residents had wanted to discuss something of importance with her (p. 130). Obviously she could not handle all three situations simultaneously by herself. Other studies report victims describing shelter staff as insensitive or neglectful, rather than empowering and caring, possibly a result of their being burned-out and overburdened (Surtees, 2007b).

Donors should be careful about how funding is provided for shelters. If care is not taken, the funding mechanism itself can contribute to a reduction in the quality of services. In Bosnia, a system of funding shelters on a per person per night basis was instituted. While this ensured that expenses were limited, it also meant that when the population of residents at the shelter was low, shelters did not have enough funding to pay for even basic costs (rent, utilities, staff, etc.). As a result some shelters operated without full-time, properly qualified personnel (Rosenberg 2006). This type of funding mechanism also provides an incentive for keeping victims in shelters rather than empowering them to transition to independence.

Funding

There are three basic ways to make services sustainable: funding by state and local government, private donations and sponsorship, and social businesses. As donor funding is declining and local economies are growing, these options are only recently being explored. More research into these options is needed to better understand the range of creative and effective solutions available.

Funding by State and Local Government

There are many examples in the region of state and local government contributing, to varying degrees, to the establishment or operation of shelters and/or assistance programs. These include direct financial contributions for NGO service providers in Bosnia, Croatia, Georgia, Kosovo, Montenegro, Romania, Russia and Turkey; state operated shelters in Albania, Bulgaria, and Romania; donations of shelter space in Georgia, Kyrgyzstan, Macedonia, and Ukraine; the provision of security for shelters in Albania, Macedonia, and Montenegro; and other in-kind contributions in Kazakhstan and Ukraine (DOS, 2007; Rosenberg, 2006).

Funding by Private Donations & Sponsorship

In other parts of the world, corporate donors and donations from private citizens are used to fund social services. However, this is a fairly new concept in the E&E region, and while many of the documents reviewed for this chapter referred to the need to explore private donations and sponsorship as a way of funding services, no concrete examples could be found where this had successfully been accomplished. This is an area for further research.

Funding by Social Businesses

Some organizations run businesses whose profits are used to fund social services (USAID, 2007, p. 25; CRS, 2007; Rosenberg, 2006; WL, 2003). These businesses are known as "social businesses." Examples were noted in several countries, such as Bosnia, Kosovo, and Romania, but detailed information about these businesses and their long-term success could not be found. This is an area to explore for further research. Such research should examine the successes and difficulties faced in launching and operating such businesses, their impact on sustainability of services, as well as how the beneficiaries of the services participate in the businesses.

6. Community-Based Assistance

Many assistance programs in the region have one or more shelters as their core, usually located in large cities and/or border areas. All assistance provided revolves around the shelter, with the end result that it may be difficult if not impossible to obtain other services if a victim is not residing at the shelter.

However, victims may wish to settle in a wide variety of locations in the country – from urban centers to small villages. Some may wish to return to their family home which could be far from a shelter. Currently, few assistance programs meet the needs of those who do not live in or near shelters. There may be a host of reasons why staying at the shelter is not a viable or effective option for some victims of trafficking. Rules of the shelter may restrict them from working or taking their children to school, they may wish to return to their family or to live in a different city, etc. Long distances or expensive travel may preclude such victims from receiving assistance (Brunovskis & Surtees, 2007, p. 91; Surtees, 2005, p. 16). Recent studies have shown that forced shelter stays can also lead victims to decline other forms of assistance (Brunovskis & Surtees, 2007, p. 31).

There have been some attempts in the region to address these shortcomings. While little information is available on the specific shelter models or their impact so far, a few will be mentioned here as examples:

- In Bosnia, one NGO has a mobile clinic which provides follow-up care to victims and their families where they reside. The NGO encourages the staff from the local center for social work to join them in order to encourage a relationship between the family and the local social workers (Rosenberg, 2006, p. 8).
- In both Serbia and Albania, the assistance framework offers an alternative to traditional emergency shelter-style accommodation through shared, subsidized apartments (IOM, 2005b, p. 10 and the author's personal experience in Albania). Living in shared, subsidized apartments with more independence than in a traditional shelter, is an important step towards a more independent life. These models, while still in urban centers, may also be appropriate for implementation in more distant locations in the country.
- In Romania, NGOs and IOs providing repatriation and shelter-based reintegration services refer victims to NGOs in their community for longer term assistance or to provide assistance to victims wishing to return home immediately. These NGOs strive to maintain regular contact with victims for up to 12 months, providing not only services, but an opportunity to monitor the impact of programs and to prevent re-trafficking. Obviously, not all victims desire this and, for a variety of reasons, may cut off contact with service providers (Surtees, 2005, p. 486). A similar model is in effect in Serbia for victims who wish to return to their home communities (IOM, 2005a, p.10; IOM, 2005b, p. 8).

- In 2006 in Albania, regional anti-trafficking committees were established in all 12 districts of the country. One responsibility of these committees is to improve the identification and referral for assistance of victims of trafficking at the local level. One year after their establishment an assessment of the committees found that they were not working effectively. This was thought to be due to a lack of financial and human resources, a need for training and capacity building and better coordination amongst both governmental and nongovernmental stakeholders (CAII, 2007b, pp. 21-32). However, one year is not much time to be able to assess the full impact of such an initiative. Bulgaria also has local commissions (Fritz, 2006, p. 11). Such initiatives should be evaluated in the future to assess their impact on the identification and referral for assistance of victims of trafficking, as well as the possible impact on reducing the stigmatization associated with victims' integration into local communities.

State Social Services

In most countries of the region, the state has social service centers located throughout the country, which are tasked to assist vulnerable communities. These offices are responsible for registering vulnerable groups, handling disbursements of social assistance, counseling on domestic violence issues, providing child protection services and the like. However, victims of trafficking are not always included in the list of eligible persons. As well, the staff is not usually trained to provide assistance to victims of trafficking. In Russia, one report notes a lack of assistance structures for victims of trafficking, but indicates the growing network of state-sponsored crisis centers for other vulnerable groups, including one for men (Tiurukanova, 2006, p. 96).

GOOD PRACTICE: BUILD CAPACITY OF AND ENGAGE THE STATE SOCIAL SERVICE SYSTEM

A recent effort in Albania through UNICEF and USAID-funded programs to engage the state's social service system in the provision of assistance to child victims of trafficking through child protection units has demonstrated success (CAII, 2007b).

These resources could be better engaged and staff could be trained to provide assistance to VOTs (Rosenberg, 2006, p. 17; Chemonics, 2005, p. 17). Donors can play an important role in building the capacity of the State's social service system to address the needs of victims of trafficking.

7. Income Generation Opportunities

Low income has been repeatedly reported to be a push factor which increases vulnerability to the false promises of traffickers. Studies of migrants throughout this region show that most decide to migrate in order to earn a better income (Kiryan & van der Linden, 2005; Stephens & van der Linden, 2005; Ghinararu & van der Linden, 2004; Michailov, et al., 2005; Winrock, 2004c). After their escape from trafficking, they are usually still in need of earning a living – either for themselves or to support their families. Assistance programs which do not address this need for income generation are not likely to succeed. One study of victims who declined assistance found that the need to earn income was a factor in some women deciding not to participate in assistance programs because participation impeded their ability to work (Brunovskis & Surtees, 2007).

Providing income generating opportunities for victims of trafficking is a critical part of any recovery program. Income generating opportunities can begin even while victims reside in shelters and need not wait for them to move into alternative accommodation. Such programs should also be made available to victims who do not reside in shelters. Income generation programs often include entrepreneurial programs, employment programs, and cooperative businesses. Because donor funding is often used to support such programs, a brief analysis of the impact of each follows.

Entrepreneurial Programs

Entrepreneurial programs designed to encourage VOTs or their families[8] to open their own businesses need to be targeted to appropriate victim populations. Those that were originally targeted to young women exploited in prostitution met with limited success. While VOTs expressed interest in the programs and enjoyed the training courses, they did not tend to successfully open their own businesses. The program implementers felt that the VOTs were still in recovery and not able to concentrate their energies on a new business (IREX, 2003b).

In Ukraine, there has been recent success in applying the entrepreneurial model to reintegration assistance programs. Of the 119 VOTs who took the entrepreneurship course offered as a first step in participating in the entrepreneurship program, 57 opened small businesses (a total of 45 businesses, as some joined together to open businesses).[9] Of these 45 businesses, 91 percent were still in operation one to two years after starting, 145 jobs were created and the assets of the businesses had tripled. Interviews with the VOTs indicate that the business is the main source of income for the family, with the average VOT entrepreneur earning UAH 2,597, significantly higher than the average wage in Ukraine in mid-2007 of UAH 1,368 (IOM, 2007c). This demonstrates that it is possible to successfully apply micro-enterprise development programs for VOT reintegration.

It is important however, to examine more closely the success of this program, including an analysis of the package of services provided, as well as the process by which participants are selected. It is worth noting that 119 VOTs is a very small percentage of the VOTs assisted in Ukraine (from 2000 – 2007, IOM assisted 3,835 VOTs {IOM, 2007b}). The socio-demographic profile of the beneficiaries participating in the entrepreneurship program may be one reason for its success. A significant portion of identified VOTs in Ukraine are VOTs for labor exploitation. As such, this population is older, both male and female, and tend to have children and spouses to support. As well, they may arguably have suffered less psychological trauma from the trafficking experience. In fact, the successful entrepreneurs from this entrepreneurship program are 61 percent female, 39 percent male, and tend to be older, with 44 percent being between 25 and 35 and 46 percent over 35. Only 11 percent are 25 or under. Most, 72 percent, have children and 65 percent are married. Furthermore, 82 percent have completed higher education or technical education (IOM, 2007c). It is not inconceivable that this older, more stable demographic is a better target for entrepreneurship programming.

In addition to examining the target population, it is also worth noting the project design. In this successful model from Ukraine, the administrators of the program were not simply given funds to distribute and the beneficiaries in this program were not just given a grant. A training manual was developed to ensure that the entrepreneurship training was tailored specifically to the needs of victims of trafficking. Trainers from a few select NGOs with relevant experience were trained to use the specially designed training manual. These NGOs then trained the VOTs who prepared business plans. Only the most viable business plans were then selected for funding (IOM, 2007c).

Before funding entrepreneurship programs, donors should examine what types of support for microbusiness is already available in the country and find ways to link former victims of trafficking to these services rather than funding duplicative ones. In Albania for example, service providers are assisting those victims who have an interest in and aptitude for starting their own business to apply to state-supported and privately-managed micro-credit programs.[10]

Employment Programs

As noted earlier, the desire or need to earn income is often what led to victims becoming vulnerable to being trafficked and exploited in the first place. After their escape from trafficking, their need for income is usually still paramount. Finding safe and gainful employment for VOTs is an important part of any assistance program.

Implementing organizations in many countries of the region have extensive employment programs which include training to raise job-seeking skills, vocational training, internships, internship stipends, and job placement services. Some track success according to the number of beneficiaries who find employment, but most do not track long-term maintenance of employment or average earnings. Implementing agencies in Albania found that victims of trafficking require significant job placement assistance. It is not enough to provide only vocational training. Victims assisted in Albania required one-on-one assistance in identifying and applying for jobs, mentoring during the first several months of the job, as well as mediation with employers. Even with this assistance it was common for most victims to quit or be let go from several jobs before finding long-term employment.[11]

As well, some programs focus both on reintegration for VOTs and prevention of TIP, and do not distinguish employment issues for former victims of trafficking and the other clients they serve (those who are considered vulnerable to becoming VOTs). Based on an assessment of trafficking prevention programs, employment programs designed for preventing trafficking often have high post-program employment rates (Rosenberg, 2004, p. 17). Employment rates vary, but a program in Belarus serving both a reintegration and a prevention function, at mid-project had a post-internship employment rate of 71 percent (IOM, 2008, p. 4; Winrock, 2007). How well these same programs work for victims of trafficking is less well documented and for dual-use programs, it is not clear from the available statistics if employment rates are different for former victims as compared to the at-risk populations that are being served.

Good Practice: Use of State Employment Agencies

Many countries of the region have state employment agencies with offices around the country which provide not only job placement services but also free or subsidized vocational training. Donors should encourage programs which develop the use of these centers for assisting former victims of trafficking as a sustainable resource when donor funding ends.

One study noted that employment programs need to be designed carefully because in many cases VOTs were trained in skills that did not lead to viable income generation once victims returned to their rural villages (e.g., hair dressers) or were in fields where the VOTs were in direct competition for jobs with much more highly educated peers (e.g., computer training or book keeping – where victims lack the formal education of those against whom they will compete; USAID, 2007, p. 18).

Better analysis of the impact of employment programs is needed. This includes keeping disaggregated impact data in order to assess how employment programs can be best designed to meet the needs of former victims of trafficking. Their needs may be quite different from the employment assistance needed for prevention of TIP by groups considered vulnerable to trafficking, but who have not been trafficked. Donor funding is needed to support such programs as well as to encourage the use and development of state employment agencies to support former victims of trafficking in finding employment.

Cooperative Businesses

Some assistance providers have also started businesses that are run by former victims of trafficking and provide income generating opportunities for them (this is in contrast to social businesses designed to fund the shelter or assistance services themselves). In Albania, for example, victims residing in the local shelter have been involved in making handicrafts for sale at an annual craft fair, and more recently in providing catering services to the international and NGO community for meetings and events. All of the income that is generated goes directly to the former victims of trafficking who participate.[12]

8. Medical Services

To date, in many countries of the region, medical services are provided by international donors. This is obviously not sustainable and does not, even in the short-term, provide sufficient assistance to victims with chronic medical problems, when the services they receive are from a project which may end in a year or two. However, some countries are exploring or working on having the state take over the provision of medical services, often by enrolling victims of trafficking in state-supported health insurance schemes or through the provision of free services at public hospitals (DOS, 2007). Most States in this region have schemes for providing free medical services to vulnerable or indigent populations. Donors should continue to encourage States to include former victims of trafficking in these schemes.

9. Capacity Building

Training and study tours for staff providing direct assistance to victims has been a key component of several trafficking projects in the region and has included such topics as stress management and burn-out, functioning of referral systems, job development skills, entrepreneurship training, legal assistance to VOTs, and mental health assistance to trafficked persons, among others (IOM, 2005a, p. 11; IOM, 2005c, p. 17; IOM, 2006a, p. 6-8; IOM, 2007a, p. 3-5). While a systematic assessment of the impact of these training programs and study tours could not be found, there were some illustrative examples of such impact. For example, in Macedonia, study visits to countries in the region were credited with directly assisting in the development of standard operating procedures for the first shelter for national victims in the country (Moens, 2007).

Even with a strong focus on training in many programs, a lack of professional training for staff providing assistance to victims has been noted in the region (Somach & Surtees, 2005). In Central Asia, NGO staff report feeling that they do not have the necessary skills to handle the severe trauma experienced by some of their clients (Kelly 2005: 85). A lack of experience and training is especially true in regard to State social service providers in many countries, where staff functions tend to be administrative and staff do not have specialized training in issues of violence or trafficking (Chemonics, 2005, p. 15, 21; Tiurukanova, 2006, p. 96). Mentoring between State social service providers and NGOs with more experience can be a productive way of building capacity and increasing coordination.

In Albania an international NGO has trained the staff of newly established municipal child protection units to identify and assist child victims of trafficking and those at risk of trafficking. The social workers work side by side with the international NGOs' experienced staff, providing on-the-job training. As a result, the staff of these child protection units have since been integral in identifying and assisting child victims of trafficking (totaling 28 in the first year of the program) as well as those at risk of being trafficked (totaling 150 in the first year of the program). Success seems to be continuing, with a combined total of 95 children at risk of trafficking or suspected of being victims of trafficking being identified in the first three quarters of the second project year (TdH, 2007; TdH, 2008).

Many of the donor-funded training activities were, unfortunately, one-off interventions and were not designed to be sustainable. Integrating such training into existing training and education mechanisms, such as schools of social work or in-service training programs takes more effort up front, but makes the training self-sustaining in the long run. Future activities should be designed with sustainability in mind.

10. Standards, Regulations, and Monitoring of Assistance

While the types of services offered throughout the region tends to be consistent, studies have shown that not all services are of equal quality. Many studies point to vast differences in the quality of services provided by different service providers and to poor treatment of victims by some providers. Whole studies have been devoted to the potential negative impact of interventions designed to provide assistance and protection (c.f. GAATW, 2007). A lack of standards and protocols for assistance has been noted throughout the region (Surtees, 2005, p. 46; Rosenberg, 2006, p. 16, 20). Having established standards is a best practice noted in some studies (USAID, 2007). Yet, Albania is the only country in the region which the author could find had established standards of care for the treatment of victims of trafficking[13] (Council of Ministers, 2007). Standards ensure the provision of quality assistance for all and provide criteria against which services can be monitored and evaluated.

Monitoring of assistance is critical for ensuring that assistance provided to victims is safe and effective, and does not in fact harm victims rather than assist them. In many countries of the region, services are provided by NGOs and are not monitored or even licensed by the state. As a result, the NGOs are not accountable to anyone and there are no assurances of the quality of their work. Similarly, services provided by the State and through referral mechanisms under State control, are rarely monitored.

GOOD PRACTICE: DEVELOPMENT OF STANDARDS, LICENSING PROCEDURES, AND INSPECTIONS

The Albanian Government recently finalized the development of standards of assistance for victims of trafficking. All providers of assistance in the country must be licensed by the State to provide such assistance and the state inspectors will ensure adherence to the standards. While still in its early stages, this is a development worth following for replication elsewhere in the region.

A lack of regulation of assistance mechanisms can lead to mistreatment of victims of trafficking. It is important therefore to set up monitoring as well as complaint mechanisms for victim protection programs (Rosenberg, 2006; Surtees, 2007b; Brunovskis & Surtees, 2007).

The importance of monitoring is noted in a study of shelter-based services in Bosnia:

> Monitoring is essential to make sure that all of the agencies and organizations involved are undertaking their roles effectively and to an acceptable standard of care. Monitoring should include ensuring that staff have the necessary professional background and level of experience and conducting examinations of individual cases to ensure that the individuals received appropriate and timely medical care, psycho-social assistance, legal assistance, documentation, or repatriation. Monitoring can also assess whether State actors are implementing their roles appropriately and effectively. The monitoring team can also assess whether the referral mechanisms in place are working or need to be revised (Rosenberg, 2006, p. 18).

Donor funding would be well put toward the development of standards for assistance as well as on monitoring mechanisms and regulatory frameworks for ensuring standards are adhered to. Donors can also make sure that programs they fund include both internal and external monitoring and evaluation mechanisms.

GOOD PRACTICE: INTERNAL MONITORING OF SERVICES

In Georgia, USAID's implementing partner developed questionnaires to be filled out by shelter and service recipients to determine how services were being provided and how these services met the needs and expectations of the recipients. They followed these up with interviews and site visits (GYLA 2007a: 6).

C. Legal Proceedings as They Relate to Victims

Threats against victims who choose to cooperate with law enforcement and testify against traffickers are real and the benefits of testifying have so far been few. Programs to improve witness protection and increase the compensation paid to victims would go a long way in securing victims' voluntary cooperation, resulting in better reporting and conviction rates.

1. Witness Protection

Many countries in the region have provisions in law for providing witness protection. These laws include a variety of interventions from physical protection to alternative methods of testifying to relocation and changes in identity. Because these provisions are mostly new, the mechanisms as well as the funding for implementation are lacking (Limanowska, 2007, p. 71; Snajdrova & Hancilova, 2007, p. 22; Tiurukanova, 2006, p. 95). Donor funding could be used to reform legislation where necessary and improve implementation of the laws.

Reducing the Negative Impacts of Testifying on Victims

Participation in trials can be very demanding and can have severe negative impacts on victims. Trials tend to be very lengthy, often dragging on for years, while the victim remains in "protective custody," restricted to life in a shelter and unable to begin the transition to normalcy. As well, victims are often forced to confront their trafficker, both formally in the courtroom and often informally and with fewer protections, in the courthouse waiting to be called for testimony. Victims are required to frequently retell the story of what happened to them, re-traumatizing them. Trials in many countries are also open to the public and the media, putting the victims at risk of being exposed publicly (see below).

Some efforts have been made to try to reduce the negative impacts of testifying. For example, in many countries, alternative mechanisms for testifying are available by law. In Serbia, this has been put to use effectively – see text box.

GOOD PRACTICE: ALTERNATIVE MECHANISMS FOR TESTIFYING

In Serbia, the testimony of two foreign victims of trafficking was filmed prior to their repatriation, negating their need to stay in Serbia until the trial was complete and allowing them to return home sooner. This did not seem to negatively effect the trial. The suspects were found guilty and sentenced to prison terms ranging from three to eight years and their property confiscated (IOM 2005a, 8; IOM 2005d: 3).

In Macedonia, this mechanism was also successfully used in one case, whereby the victim-witness gave video testimony from a courthouse in her country of residence. The video was set up in the courtroom in Macedonia in such a way as the defendant and the public could only hear her testimony while the other principals could see it as well (Velkoska, 2005, p. 41).

In some countries of the region, victims are also protected by law from confronting the trafficker in the court building before the trial by the provision of a separate room to hold the victim-witness prior to testifying. Sadly, the physical space of the courtrooms and buildings do not always allow for proper implementation of the law (Velkoska, 2005, p. 44). Similarly, in some countries of the region, there are now provisions in law that allow the judge to exclude the public from the trial. In Macedonia, this has in some cases been successfully applied, but in others the request for a closed trial was denied or such a trial was never requested (Velkoska, 2005, p. 28).

Problems with implementation of such laws to protect victim-witnesses during court proceedings remain the case in many countries in this region. The laws have been modified to allow for such alternative ways of testifying and protecting the victim-witnesses, but the mechanisms are used in very few cases. Encouraging further use of such mechanisms is still needed.

Protection of Identity

The United Nations Protocol requires that States take measures to protect the identity of TIP victims. Yet, in many countries in the E&E region there is no law to protect victims from having their identity exposed in the media. Throughout the region there are reports of victims' names, addresses and photos being published by the media (Kelly, 2005, p. 83; IOM, 2006c, p. 3; GYLA, 2007b, p. 13).

UN PROTOCOL - ARTICLE 6 : ASSISTANCE TO AND PROTECTION OF VICTIMS OF TRAFFICKING IN PERSONS

"1. In appropriate cases and to the extent possible under its domestic law, each State Party shall protect the privacy and identity of victims of trafficking in persons, including, inter alia, by making legal proceedings relating to such trafficking confidential."

Revealing victims' identities publicly can have many negative consequences, from increasing their shame and making it more difficult to reintegrate into society to putting victims (as well as their family and associates) at risk from their traffickers, and can result in victims refusing to further cooperate with law enforcement or to access assistance services.

GOOD PRACTICE: TRAINING MEDIA TO PROTECT VICTIM IDENTITY

In Kosovo, training for journalists included a focus on the negative consequences to victims from being identified in the media. After the training, many of the journalist participants indicated in the evaluation that they would not publish identifying information about victims. They appeared to be true to their commitment as an assessment of trafficking in the media found that in the five weeks following the training not one story of trafficking in the media included photographs or identifying information (CRS 2007: 5).

Several countries have provided training to journalists, often to improve or increase their reporting on trafficking and to raise public awareness of the issue. In some countries, this has also included a component on the importance of protecting victim identity – see the Kosovo good practice text box below. In addition to such training, it is advisable to enact legislation which protects the identity of victims of crime, especially trafficking, as well as development of a code of conduct for journalists and media outlets.

Amnesty for Crimes Committed While Trafficked

Some anti-trafficking actors in the region believe that a lack of amnesty for victims who are charged for crimes which they committed while they were trafficked prevents victims from coming forward to testify (Winrock, 2004a, p. 29; Kelly, 2005, p. 88). However in most, albeit not all, countries of this region, victims are given amnesty for crimes committed while they were trafficked (DOS, 2007). In countries where this is not yet the case, efforts should be made to insert such an exclusion into the law.

In other countries it is considered a crime for a witness not to testify, thereby requiring by law that victims of trafficking cooperate with law enforcement and testify against their traffickers. This is the case in Russia (Tiurukanova, 2006, p. 94) and in Albania, where victims have been arrested for revoking their complaint of trafficking and refusing to further cooperate – even when this was done because of credible threats from the traffickers. This same law has been used to pressure caregivers to give law enforcement information provided to them by victims under a promise of confidentiality.[14]

Physical Protection

Victims of trafficking, their families and those supporting them are often under threat by traffickers, more so when the victim has agreed to cooperate with law enforcement. There are several ways in which victims, their families and support persons can be physically protected. These include:

- Police escort to and from the police station, court, etc., for the victim, his/her family and support persons.
- Provision of security at victim's place of residence, as well as that of his/her family and support persons..
- Relocation of victim (and family, when necessary and desired).
- New identification for victim (and family, when necessary and desired).

In Macedonia, in one case, a victim, her family, and the NGO staff supporting her were provided with limited protection in the form of escort to and from the court and for other meetings (OG/LS, 2007). Victims have also been provided with protection while in the court itself. However, in one case, the defendant's attorney successfully argued that the security personnel provided for the victim-witness should not be allowed in the courtroom as they could influence the victim. Without security, the victim felt much less safe testifying against the traffickers (Velkoska, 2005, p. 28).

Relocation and Change of Identity

There have been a number of cases in the region in which victims of trafficking have been relocated to third countries as a result of credible threats both in the country of destination and origin. However, these are handled mostly *ad hoc*. In Albania, the process was originally handled by a coordinating group of international organizations. However, when a witness protection law entered into force, the Albanian Government was to have taken over. Since that time, there have been no successful third country relocations, although international organizations are still seeking such solutions for some victims.[15] In Bosnia, one relocation was initiated by the Prosecutor, but with the assistance of an international organization. The traffickers in this case were convicted and a follow-up study of the relocated victim-witnesses demonstrated that the relocation did result in a durable solution (Limanowska, 2007, p.71).

UN PROTOCOL - ARTICLE 6 : ASSISTANCE TO AND PROTECTION OF VICTIMS OF TRAFFICKING IN PERSONS

"5. Each State Party shall endeavour to provide for the physical safety of victims of trafficking in persons while they are within its territory."

Developing systematic approaches for relocations is important. Bilateral agreements need to be developed which will allow for international relocations, since many countries of the region are too small to make a change of identity feasible.

2. Compensation

A victim's right to legal avenues to pursue compensation is provided by international law. In many countries of the region there are several legal mechanisms through which victims can claim compensation for lost wages as well as pain and suffering: through the criminal proceedings, through the civil courts, through victim compensation funds, and through administrative procedures and mediated settlements. However, the number of compensation claims made and awarded is very small compared to the number of victims (even just counting those who are identified, and not including the many that are never identified as trafficked). As well, while in many countries of the region States have the legal possibility to seize trafficker's assets to pay such claims, ensuring enforcement and payment of claims is fraught with difficulties (Thompson & Jernow, 2008).

Compensation through Criminal Proceedings

In some countries, courts can award restitution as part of a criminal case. In this scenario, the burden of gathering and presenting evidence is removed from the victim. However, in order for such awards to be made, there has to be a successful criminal case, of which there are very few. Also, in some countries, restitution may only be provided for material damages and may not cover non-material damages, thus lowering the awards. Prosecutors may also be reluctant to attach such compensation claims to their criminal cases as it may make the victim appear to be a less reliable witness, one who has a financial motive for testifying. In the United States, procedures have been established that get around this argument by making it obligatory for the prosecutor to make a restitution claim in trafficking cases as well as in cases of other violent crimes (Thompson & Jernow, 2008).

Compensation through Civil Claims

Civil claims for compensation can be made through criminal or civil proceedings, depending on the laws of the country. When appended to criminal proceedings, the advantage is that the prosecutor takes on responsibility for gathering and presenting the evidence, so that the burden is not on the victim. Some of the problems with these cases are that; 1) judges may see the civil claim as secondary to the criminal case and may not give it proper consideration, and 2) the civil claim is contingent upon a criminal conviction. There are many reasons why a criminal case may be dropped or the defendant acquitted, which are not related to the defendant's guilt or innocence. This would result in the victim's compensation claim also being dropped (Thompson & Jernow, 2008).

UN Protocol - Article 6 : Assistance to and Protection of Victims of Trafficking in Persons

"6. Each State Party shall ensure that its domestic legal system contains measures that offer victims of trafficking in persons the possibility of obtaining compensation for damage suffered."

Civil claims through civil proceedings are generally allowable in this region, but are used infrequently in trafficking cases. The full burden of gathering and presenting evidence is on the victim. The process can be very time-consuming, expensive and complicated and few cases have actually resulted in victims receiving compensation (Chemonics, 2005, p. 9, 19; Velkoska, 2005, p. 49; Apap & Medved, 2003; Thompson & Jernow, 2008).

Compensation through Administrative Procedures/Mediated Settlements

Because of the difficulty in claiming and receiving compensation, alternatives to criminal or civil suits have also been utilized. Pursuing compensation through labor law or other administrative procedures is one mechanism available in some countries. Often such procedures may be easier to pursue than through the criminal or civil courts. They may also be more palatable options for victims who do not see themselves as victims of trafficking or do not wish to pursue criminal sanctions, but who would be interested in seeking claims for lost wages or other damages. In countries where the labor inspectorate is strong and has sufficient resources and power, they can be very effective in pursuing compensation (see text box for examples from the United States). However, such options may not be available for all victims of trafficking. Labor law procedures may not be available if the work in which the victim was engaged was illegal (such as prostitution or begging), or if the workers are irregular migrants (Thompson & Jernow, 2008).

Good Practice: Use of Administrative Procedures

The US Dept of Labor (USDOL) and the US Equal Opportunities Commission (EEOC) have been very successful in obtaining compensation in labor exploitation and trafficking cases. For example, in 2004, USDOL negotiated a settlement of US$1.9 million for 775 employees of a janitorial services company. In a landmark case in American Samoa, USDOL obtained back wages of US$367,000 and fined the company US$213,000 in penalties on behalf of 213 employees (Thompson & Jernow, 2008). EEOC obtained US$1 million settlement in a case involving Thai workers at a steel plant. In another case EEOC obtained over 1.2 million for 52 Indian nationals working at a U.S. factory.

Mediated settlements can also be effective mechanisms for obtaining compensation for victims of trafficking. In some countries, NGOs, labor unions or even government administrative bodies, can negotiate with the exploiters to pay compensation to their victims. In Russia, the Construction Workers Union has had success in pressuring employers to pay owed wages for work-related injuries in order to avoid going to court (Thompson & Jernow, 2008). While such mechanisms have been most effective in labor cases, given the difficulty in getting compensation paid through other means, methods to expand the use of mediation should be explored.

Compensation through Victim Compensation Funds

In some countries, the State provides compensation through a state compensation fund. Such schemes have the distinct advantage that the trafficker does not have to be identified or located for a claim to be made. As well, the procedures for making a claim are generally significantly less complex than pursuing a case in a court of law and problems of enforcement are avoided. Usually, however, claims paid by victim compensation funds are less than would be awarded by a court (Thompson & Jernow, 2008). Such funds are being developed in many countries of the region, but so far have been under-funded and under-utilized.

Good Practice: Victim Compensation Funds

The United Kingdom (UK) has a well developed victim compensation scheme, which, until recently, had provisions which made it difficult for victims of trafficking to make claims. However, in a recent case, victims of trafficking for prostitution have been awarded between 16,500 – 62,000 British pounds from the Criminal Injuries Compensation Authority, under a new interpretation of their guidelines. For the first time, the Authority will pay compensation for "false imprisonment and forced prostitution during the time of their imprisonment" (Townsend 2007).

Difficulties in Pursing Compensation Claims

Even in countries known for having a well established rule of law, and where compensation claims can be made during the course of the criminal proceedings, several studies explain some of the reasons why victims of trafficking may not pursue compensation claims: lack of information about their right to claim compensation, lack of legal support to make claims, lack of confidence in the legal system, fear of adverse consequences from the traffickers or a desire to break all ties with the trafficker (Dettmeijer-Vermeulen *et al.,* 2008, p. 128-129; Thompson & Jernow, 2008). Given the frequency with which traffickers in this region receive limited or suspended sentences (c.f. DOS, 2007), victims' fears of adverse consequences for testifying against them, let alone for suing them for compensation, are not unfounded.

Other problems in awarding compensation to victims of trafficking come from complications in calculating the basis of damages. In many countries of the region, awarding of damages for pain and suffering is a new concept, and, as such, legal practitioners may have no experience or basis for calculating such awards (Velkoska, 2005, p. 50-51; Thompson & Jernow, 2008). As well, for cases of labor exploitation there may be a clear basis in the labor laws for calculating lost wages, but calculating damages for those forced into exploitation, which does not fall within the labor laws, may be more complicated. In most of the countries of this region, prostitution is illegal and therefore not covered under the labor laws of the country. This may impact on the ability or willingness of the court to calculate and award damages.[16] The U.S. has gotten around this by using a broader definition of lost income to include the "value to the defendant of the victim's services or labor," thus providing a basis for calculating lost income even in cases where the labor was illegal, and depriving the perpetrators of the illegal profits (Thompson & Jernow, 2008, p. 136).

Even when compensation is awarded, ensuring the enforcement of such claims is very difficult. Lengthy delays in criminal proceedings are commonplace in the region, giving the defendant more time to hide or transfer ownership of assets. Due to the transnational nature of many cases, the trafficker may not be within the jurisdiction of the case or the victim may have already left the country in which the claim can be made. Similarly, the trafficker may not have assets from which to pay compensation or the State may not have sufficient resources to confiscate such assets as do exist.

Good Practice: Victim Compensation

- *Bosnia: In a recent case, the judge ordered seizure of the trafficker's apartment and payment of compensation to the victim in the amount of $62,500 (interview with the State Coordinator's office).*
- *In Tajikistan a judge awarded a victim of trafficking ownership of an apartment owned by the trafficker (Kelly, 2005, p. 83).*
- *In Macedonia, as of September 2005, there had been two successful compensation claims, with 98,023 denars (approximately US$2,500) being awarded for material damages (Velkoska, 2005, p. 51-52).*
- *In Ukraine, compensation of UAH 20,000 (3,000 Euro or approximately US$ 4,500) was awarded to two victims of trafficking (Thompson & Jernow, 2008, p. 105).*

Even in the United States, where victims have been awarded substantial claims, enforcement of these claims has been less successful, with many victims never receiving the compensation to which they are entitled (Thompson & Jernow, 2008).

Why Compensation is Important

Awarding compensation to victims is critical. Not only will the possibility of receiving compensation be an incentive for victims to testify against traffickers, but it also eases their reintegration, empowers the victim, and relieves the State of some of the cost of reintegration as the victim will have access to funds to assist in his/her own recovery, paying for further education, starting a small business, etc. It is important that these mechanisms be in place and be further supported. There have been a few notable cases in the region where victims have been awarded some form of compensation. (See the text box for some examples.) While these awards are small, they are a start and should be encouraged. In order to further compensation for victims of trafficking, a range of interventions should be supported, such as:

- Establishing mechanisms for pursing claims which minimize the burden on victims of trafficking;
- Making pursuit of compensation obligatory by prosecutors so that a victim's credibility as a witness is not compromised by requesting compensation;
- Strengthening relevant administrative bodies, such as labor inspectorates;
- Developing the means for negotiated settlements;
- Making the provision of information to victims about their right to claim compensation obligatory and providing such information in writing.

D. Monitoring and Evaluation of Assistance Programs

Monitoring of programs is not only important for USAID to understand the impact of the projects it funds, but is important to ensure that assistance provided to victims is safe and effective, and does not in fact harm victims rather than assist them. The importance of setting up systems for monitoring direct assistance is described in Section B-10.

For all donors it is important that the desired results are clearly articulated and that there are clear indicators to measure success. While most USAID projects track indictors, most of the indicators which tracked victim protection were output oriented (e.g., number of persons assisted) and did not measure impact of programs (e.g., the number of victims still employed one year after receiving vocational training). This has been the case in nearly all of the protection programs reviewed for this chapter. The Tool Kit for Designing Trafficking Protection Programs (Annex B) includes clearly articulated results for different programmatic areas, suggested interventions to achieve these results, justification for the interventions suggested, and sample indicators to measure the impact of the interventions and the achievement of the results. These can be adapted to the local context and applied to new or ongoing programs.

There are many difficulties in assessing the impact of protection programs, especially when it comes to direct assistance for victims. One difficulty is determining how success is defined. The other is the time frame in which success is measured. These are discussed below.

Defining Success

There are some studies which have shown that victims and those providing assistance to them may have different definitions of successful (re)integration. For example, assistance providers may define success as the victim not attempting to migrate again (Brunovskis & Surtees, 2007). The victim may define success as migrating, finding a good job abroad and being able to send money home. Researchers have found that, in general, returned migrants, including trafficked persons, wished to work abroad again, regardless of their trafficking experiences the first time around – which often included violence and many other human rights abuses. Specifically, in Ukraine, 60 percent of trafficked persons interviewed wished to go abroad again (Kiryan & van der Linden, 2005, p. 42); in Romania, 78 percent (Ghinararu & van der Linden, 2004, p. 42) and in Albania, fully 93 percent of those interviewed desired to go abroad again (Stephens & van der Linden, 2005, p. 34). Therefore, defining what is meant by success for direct assistance programs can be very difficult.

Assessing the Time Frame

There is a need to follow-up with beneficiaries to see how they benefited from the services provided (USAID, 2007). Different programs use different time frames to measure the success of reintegration – from as few as three months to three years (Somach & Surtees, 2005). Longer time frames are of more interest and demonstrate more impact, but are complicated by the length of donor funding as well as the implementing organization's ability to maintain contact with the victims, who may have moved, changed telephone numbers, married and changed their name, or simply do not wish to be contacted.

Regardless of the inherent difficulties, more can be done that would better assess the impact of programs. Donors and others who fund these programs need to ensure that the indicators which are selected demonstrate impact and are not only output oriented. Annex B: Tool Kit for Designing Trafficking Protection Programs can assist donors in this process.

E. Quantifying Trafficking

The ultimate objective of anti-trafficking efforts is to reduce the amount of trafficking and the number of people trafficked. Therefore, analyzing the impact of such efforts necessarily requires that one is able to estimate the number of victims of trafficking. Research can also be used to contradict popular myths – myths that could lead to more people being trafficked because they believe these falsehoods and are unaware of the true dynamics of trafficking (Watson, 2005d, p. 8). Research can also be used to influence government action especially if the government has been unwilling to recognize the problem of trafficking and the research makes a compelling case that it is a significant problem. Yet quantifying the number of victims of trafficking is fraught with difficulties, such as differences in definitions and criteria used, lack of mechanisms to share data, the hidden nature of the population, different methodologies for extrapolating numbers, inconsistency and reliability of data, etc. (GAO, 2007, p. 21; Kutnik, Belser & Danailova-Trainor, 2007).

In the following sections, we will examine possible methodologies as well as the difficulties inherent in quantifying the number of victims of TIP who are identified and assisted and methods of extrapolating from known data to determine trafficking prevalence rates.

1. Victims Identified and Assisted

Quantifying the number of TIP victims who are identified and assisted would seem to be a reasonable undertaking and provides useful information, although it does not tell us anything about the actual magnitude of trafficking in a country or region. Increases in the numbers of TIP victims who are identified could signify improvements in identification efforts rather than an increase in trafficking. The opposite is also true. Decreases in the number of victims identified could signify a decline in the overall trafficking rates, but it could equally represent a decline in identification efforts.

National Databases

There is a lack of good data on trafficking in many countries in the region. Before the development of national databases the Regional Clearing Point (RCP) was a mechanism established to "contribute to and ensure high-quality protection and assistance services to trafficking victims through the collection, analysis and cross-referencing of national and regional data on the trafficking phenomenon and the victim assistance and protection programs currently in place" (IOM, 2005b, p. 4). The reports from the RCP provided the first comprehensive analysis of trafficking trends in the region, based on the experience of identified victims. However, the project ended with the end of donor funding.

Since then, many donors have worked with countries to develop national databases, some dedicated to trafficking and others integrated into other databases such as for border management or crime statistics. These databases would help to consolidate national data, collected according to standard criteria. As noted above, these databases will only provide information about the identified victim population and will still not tell us about the potential demographics or needs of those who do not come to the attention of authorities or assistance providers, nor will it tell us about the magnitude of trafficking in the country.

While information about the impact of these database programs could not be found, there are concerns about national databases that will need to be addressed. For example, in some countries only those victims who cooperate with law enforcement are included in the national database. Disagreements may arise as to who qualifies as a victim of trafficking. Victims may be double counted if they seek assistance from more than one service provider. The protection of data is of concern to make sure victims'identity is protected and that the information is not used against them – by law enforcement, employers, or others.

Table 2. Number of Romanian Victims Identified in Country of Origin as Compared to a Country of Destination

Data of Romanian VOTs exploited in the Netherlands	2003	2004
Number of VOTs Reported by the Dutch Rapporteur	31	45
Number of VOTs Reported by the RCP	2	1

Sources: Dettmeijer-Vermeulen *et al.* 2008: 255 and Surtees 2005: 453

Table 3. Number of Bulgarian Victims Identified in Country of Origin as Compared to a Country of Destination

Data for Bulgarian VOTs exploited in the Netherlands	2003	2004
Number of VOTs Reported by the Dutch Rapporteur	48	55
Number of VOTs Reported by the RCP	4	6

Sources: Dettmeijer-Vermeulen *et al.* 2008: 253 and Surtees 2005: 180

Table 4. Number of Ukrainian Victims Identified in Country of Compared to a Country of Destination

Data for Ukrainian VOTs exploited in the Netherlands	2001	2002	2003	2004	2005
Number of VOTs Reported by the Dutch Rapporteur	18	5	14	8	10
Number of VOTs Reported by IOM	0	5	1	0	3

Sources: Dettmeijer-Vermeulen *et al.* 2008: 255 and IOM 2007b: 1

While it is generally recognized that the numbers of victims actually identified is undoubtedly significantly lower than the actual victim population, it is also important to remember that even reports of identified and assisted victims are in all likelihood significantly under estimating the total number of identified victims. It is interesting to note for example, that data is often not consolidated across countries so that numbers of victims reported by countries of origin usually do not include victims identified and assisted in countries of destination – especially when those victims either do not return to their country of origin or return without notification of authorities or referral to assistance providers.[17]

One can see from comparing the data on identified victims of trafficking reported by the Dutch Rapporteur with consolidated data reported from the Regional Clearing Point for Southeastern Europe (RCP) that the consolidated data did not include those of the Dutch Rapporteur. In fact, the RCP had difficulty in obtaining data from many destination countries with the end result that the total estimated number of identified VOTs reported by the RCP, and by the government and civil society of the countries of origin (from which the RCP also gathered data) must be significantly underreported[18]

As can be seen from the data above, for the Netherlands, Bulgaria is one of largest source countries for victims of trafficking, with 48 VOTs from Bulgaria in 2003 and 55 in 2006. Yet, these victims are clearly not recorded in the consolidated data in Bulgaria. In fact, according to the RCP data, in 2003 there were only four Bulgarian VOTs to the Netherlands, and six VOTs in 2004. Even if it is assumed that the victims reported in the Bulgaria data are included in the data from the Netherlands (which they may not be), there are still 44 identified victims from 2003 and 49 from 2004 who are not included in the Bulgarian national data. In 2003, Bulgaria reported a total of 159 victims of trafficking for sexual exploitation (Surtees, 2005, 180). If the 44 unreported VOTs from the Netherlands are added in, the number increases by nearly 28 percent to 203. If the data from the Netherlands is so underreported in the Bulgarian data, how much is the total Bulgarian national data underreported when all countries of destination are taken into consideration? If data from all countries of destination is equally unlikely to make its way back to the countries of origin, it becomes clear that data from countries of origin significantly underreports even the number of identified victims. This does not take into consideration the number of victims who are never identified.[19]

A new program in Southeast Europe has developed two distinct trafficking databases at the national level – one which tracks victim data and the other, which is law enforcement focused, tracks trafficker and crime data. The purpose of developing these databases was to 'contribute to the harmonization and improved quality and reliability of data related to trafficking in persons' in the Southeastern Europe region (Surtees, 2007a, p. 11). However, each database is nationally owned and the sharing of data across countries will be determined on an individual level. It is too early to assess the impact of this new project, but it will be interesting to see if this can serve as a model for improved transnational data sharing.

2. Trafficking Prevalence Rates

Several studies in the region have attempted to estimate the prevalence of trafficking. An IOM-funded study in 2006 provides estimates of human trafficking in Belarus, Bulgaria, Moldova, Romania and Ukraine, based on nationally representative surveys. Survey participants were asked about their own experiences as well as those of their families and close associates which resemble situations of trafficking. The prevalence was then extrapolated to the larger population. This led to some interesting findings including prevalence rates that far exceed the number of identified victims of trafficking, and the fact that trafficking prevalence rates were not always linked to labor migration rates (meaning that higher rates of labor migration did not necessarily predict higher rates of trafficking {IOM, 2006b}). Other studies have also utilized innovative methods to attempt to quantify the number of victims of trafficking, including key informant surveys (c.f. Hampton & Ball, 2008, MSI 2004), capture re-capture (c.f. Belser, de Cock & Mehran, 2005) and household surveys.

In recent years, in some countries there is an assumption that the problem of trafficking has been addressed. However, this assumption is based on a reduction in the number of identified victims of trafficking, which some people believe is a result more of reductions in the frequency and effectiveness of police raids, and of trafficking being pushed underground. Properly conducted research would be a more reliable way of ascertaining whether or not human trafficking continues to be an issue or whether past programs have had an impact.

Note: A number of public opinion surveys have been conducted in the region which also attempt to quantify trafficking. While public opinion surveys can be very helpful in assessing public knowledge about trafficking and prevention, they should not be used to assess the nature or dynamics of trafficking. The public's opinions about trafficking are generally formed by what they hear in the media. Their opinions can, therefore, promote common assumptions – such as only women are vulnerable to trafficking or that trafficking is primarily for the purpose of prostitution. Many research studies have shown these assumptions to be untrue. Surveys of the public that ask about respondents' personal migration experiences, such as the one described above, are more appropriate for assessing trafficking prevalence.

F. Trafficking Program Management and Design

Short-term Funding

One of the problems inherent in the design of many trafficking programs is their short-term nature. Expecting to achieve significant impact and sustainability of services in a short time is not realistic. Not only does short-term funding put a strain on service providers who have to spend significantly more time raising funds, but it also limits their ability to monitor the impact of the programs and to provide continuous services for victims.

It is not only difficult to have an impact with short-term funding, but it also does not provide enough time in which to measure the sustainability of the impact. For example, with one year funding a project could provide vocational training to VOTs, although they would be limited to vocational training which could be completed in less than one year. They could measure the number of VOTs who were successfully employed immediately after taking the course, so long as they were able to obtain the job quickly after finishing the course. They would not be able to measure the number who found employment after the funding ended. They would also not be able to follow-up with the VOTs to see if six months or 12 months later they still had employment and if this employment brought them a satisfactory income. They would not know if some of those they assisted had not been able to find satisfactory employment or may have been re-trafficked as a result of taking risks in the hopes of finding the better life they dreamed of and which the assistance did not help them to achieve.

Too Many Partners / Sub-Grants

Too many partners with too many small grants can result in programs which are inappropriately focused and leave little time or money for capacity building or proper management and oversight of sub-grants (for an example, see Watson, 2005b, p. 9).

Combining Prevention with (Re) Integration

It is interesting to note that many of the reintegration services offered in the region, especially employment and entrepreneurship programs, are offered as both reintegration programs for VOTs and prevention programs for a defined vulnerable target group. This is an interesting approach as it provides for a range of assistance to VOTs without identifying them as VOTs since the programs are open to a wider audience. It also integrates VOTs with the general population, not only reducing stigma, but also easing the way toward normalized relations with the "outside" world.

V. Recommendations

This section summarizes the recommendations which come from the analysis of protection programs as described in Section IV above and are presented in that same order. Therefore, they should not be read as in order of priority. For more information about the justification and reasoning behind the recommendations please refer to the corresponding sub-section of section IV above. For specific details of how programs can be designed to incorporate these recommendations, please see Annex B: Tool Kit for Designing Trafficking Protection Programs.

A. Identification

1. Improve and expand identification efforts. Raise awareness amongst anti-trafficking actors that victims of trafficking can include men, women and children, of all ages, nationalities and ethnicities, trafficked for a wide range of exploitative purposes.
2. Improve identification as well as referral for assistance by law enforcers, border officials, consular officers and others by providing training but also through the development and implementation of clear operational procedures.
3. Increase efforts to reduce stigma and misconceptions about trafficking amongst both the public and anti-trafficking actors in order to reduce the shame in being identified as a victim of trafficking.
4. Support hotlines and awareness-raising campaigns to increase the use of hotlines for reporting cases of trafficking and identification of victims. Fund awareness-raising campaigns with which victims and their families will identify, avoid violent or provocative imagery and the use of off-putting terms such as victim, trafficking, and prostitution.
5. Increase identification of VOTs and referral by clients of prostitution by targeting awareness-raising campaigns to this group. Link these campaigns to a hotline where informants can anonymously report cases. Similar efforts can be attempted for other types of trafficking; targeting the public, for example, in areas where migrant construction workers or domestic workers are known to work.
6. Avoid funding duplicate hotlines and be sure to link all awareness-raising campaigns to existing hotlines.
7. Use care in funding organizations to implement hotlines to ensure that these organizations have the necessary skills and experience because hotline operations can be dangerous for everyone involved.
8. Expand opportunities to develop bilateral and transnational relationships between origin and destination countries in order to expand identification and improve cross-border referrals.

B. Assistance

1. Design programs for all potential victim populations – men, women and children, individuals who are trafficked for prostitution, labor, begging, etc.
2. Structure assistance programs to meet not only the basic needs of victims of trafficking, but also to assist them in achieving their aspirations.
3. Ensure that a functional referral mechanism is in place that prioritizes victims and is based on the voluntary and informed participation of VOTs.
4. Develop mechanisms for monitoring the implementation of referral mechanisms and assistance provision.
5. Develop materials which can be used to inform victims about the assistance options available to them.
   a. In countries of origin, materials should be developed for potential victims of trafficking prior to their departure informing them of assistance available in key destination countries and providing contact details abroad and at home.
   b. In countries of origin, materials should also be developed which inform potential victims of trafficking on their return home of their rights and of the assistance available to them, by all assistance providers in the country. This should be made available to all returning migrants, but especially those who are deported, returning without documents, or returning under other unusual circumstances.
   c. In countries of destination, materials should be developed which inform victims of trafficking upon identification of their rights and of the assistance options available to them and should be in available in the main languages spoken by VOTs and migrants in the country.
6. Donors should take care in funding shelter services. They should make a careful assessment of the existing shelter services in the country and take care not to fund duplicative services.
7. Donors should encourage the development of monitoring mechanisms to ensure that victims' rights are not violated in the provision of services and that victims' rights take precedence over those of the State or law enforcement.

8. Donors should encourage cost-sharing mechanisms with the state or local government. Encourage the development of other cost sharing mechanisms, but take care that such mechanisms as well as cost-cutting measures do not negatively impact on services or cause violations of the rights of victims.
9. Encourage income generation activities for victims of trafficking, including employment programs, development of cooperative businesses and even entrepreneurship when appropriate. Develop linkages to existing state and private mechanisms in the country so as to encourage sustainability: for example, through state employment offices or private micro-credit schemes.
10. Encourage states to provide free medical services for victims of trafficking by including them in state-funded insurance or medical services schemes.
11. Ensure sustainability of training programs (e.g. for police, teachers, social workers, etc.) by funding training which is integrated into existing academic, pre-service or in-service training programs.
12. Encourage the development of mechanisms to monitor TIP victim referral procedures and assistance programs. Monitoring is essential to ensure that the referral mechanisms are implemented as intended, that minimum standards of care are being utilized, and that the victims' rights are being respected. Complaint mechanisms, which are clear and easy to understand and use, should be incorporated into every program.

C. Legal Proceedings Related to Victims

1. Encourage the use of alternative methods of testifying against traffickers where they already exist in law to protect TIP victims and lessen the burden on them of cooperating with justice. In places where such alternatives do not yet exist, donors could fund programs to reform the legislation to allow for them, as well as to then encourage their use.
2. Develop legislation to protect TIP victims' identity by making it illegal for media or others to release identifying information about victims to the public. Training and development of codes of ethics for journalists can also be encouraged.

3. In countries where it is not yet the case, encourage reform of legislation to provide amnesty for crimes that were committed while victims were trafficked.
4. Develop programs to reform legislation to ensure that caregivers or other service providers for VOTs are exempted from testifying in court or providing to law enforcement information given to them by their clients.
5. Develop programs to encourage the physical protection of TIP victim-witnesses, their families, and those who are assisting them.
6. Develop mechanisms for TIP victims to claim compensation from traffickers or to receive compensation from the State. Fund programs designed to encourage the implementation and use of these mechanisms to pay compensation in order to set a precedent for the future.

D. Monitoring and Evaluation of Assistance Programs

1. Ensure that monitoring mechanisms are in place to measure program impact as well as to ensure that no harm is caused by donor-funded programs which are being improperly implemented.
2. Develop and monitor the use of impact indicators for all elements of anti-TIP programs (refer to Annex B: Tool Kit for Designing Trafficking Protection Programs).

E. Quantifying Trafficking

1. Encourage data sharing between countries of origin and countries of destination in order to ensure that data on identified TIP victims is as accurate and all-encompassing as possible.
2. Encourage funding for trafficking prevalence studies as a way of measuring changes in trafficking over time. Such studies can appropriately be used in countries where long-term interventions have taken place to measure impact or to encourage government action in places where there is doubt about the current state of trafficking in the country.

F. Trafficking Program Management and Design

1. Fund long-term anti-TIP projects (three to five years), rather than short-term projects.
2. Do not spread money and resources too thinly by trying to provide too many sub-grants to all possible stakeholders.
3. Combine the provision of services for vulnerable groups with those for former victims of trafficking. This has the possibility of reducing the stigma associated with trafficking by allowing trafficked persons to blend with other populations. This can be done by combining prevention and protection programs or by integrating trafficked persons as beneficiaries into non-trafficking programs, for example, by assisting trafficked persons to apply for micro-credit programs designed for the general population. It is important, however, that impact data be disaggregated to better assess the impact of the projects on the different categories of program participants and to help ascertain if programs need to be adapted in some way to be more effective for trafficked persons.

ANNEX A. REFERENCES

Academy for Educational Development (AED) (n.d.). *Prevention of Trafficking and Protection of Victims of Violence.* Replicable Approaches: A Guide. The Academy for Educational Development: Washington.

Apap, Joanna & Medved, Felicita. (2003). *Protection Schemes for Victims of Trafficking in Selected EU Member Countries, Candidate and Third Countries.* International Organization for Migration: Geneva.

Armenia Sociological Association. (2005). *Trafficking and Labour Exploitation of Armenian Migrants: A Sociological Survey.* ASA: Yerevan.

Bedelbayeva, Aidai. (2005). *Preventing Human Trafficking in Kyrgyzstan Project: Project Evaluation Report.* Winrock International, November 2005.

Belser, Patrick, de Cock Michaelle, & Mehran, Farhad. (2005). *ILO Minimum Estimate of Forced labour in the World.* International Labour Office: Geneva.

Blumberg, Rae Lesser and Shved, Olha. (2002). *Curbing Sex Slavery Abroad by Helping Women Earn a Living in Ukraine: An Assessment of the Economic Empowerment Aspects of the Anti-Trafficking Project,* USAID/Kiev. Development Alternatives, Inc. & USAID Office of Women in Development: Washington.

Brunovskis, Anette & Surtees, Rebecca. (2007). *Leaving the Past Behind: When Victims of Trafficking Decline Assistance.* Fafo (Oslo) and Nexus Institute (Vienna).

Callender, Elizabeth, Esquibel, Theresa, Sewall, Rebecca & Zollner, Anne. (2003). Mid-term Evaluation of the USDOL/IREX Regional Empowerment Initiative for Women. November 2002 – February 2003. Management Systems International.: Washington.

Catholic Relief Services. (2007). *Partnership Against Trafficking in Human Beings: Quarterly Report January 1, 2007 – March 31, 2007.* Catholic Relief Services: Kosovo.

CHEMONICS. (2005). *Serbia and Montenegro Anti-Trafficking Assessment: February 28 – March 12, 2005.* Chemonics International, Inc.

CHEMONICS. (2007). *Anti Trafficking Technical Assistance: Annual Progress Report October 1, 2005 – September 30, 2006.* Chemonics International, Inc.: Washington.

Council of Ministers. (2007). National Standards of Services for Trafficked Persons or for Persons at Risk of Trafficking Accommodated in Residential Centres in Albania. Council of Ministers: Tirana.

Creative Associates International, Inc. (CAII). (2007a). CAAHT - An Integrated Management Information System Plan for FY 2007 -2009. CAII: Washington.

CAII. (2007b). *The State of Efforts to Combat Trafficking of Persons in Albania – August 2006 to July 2007.* October 2007. Creative Associates International, Inc.: Tirana.

CAII. (2006). *CAAHT – FY 2006 Annual Work Plan Progress Report.* Creative Associates International, Inc.: Tirana.

U.S. Department of Justice. (2007). *Assessment of U.S. Government Efforts to Combat Trafficking in Persons.* September 2007.

Dettmeijer-Vermeulen, C. E. with Boot-Matthijssen, M., van Dijk, E.M.H., de Jonge van Ellemeet, H., Koster, D. A. C. & M. Smit. (2008). *Trafficking in Human Beings: Fifth Report of the Dutch National Rapporteur.*

EnCOMPASS. (2007). Comprehensive Report of Assessment Visit to CAAHT/Albania in February 2007 and Recommendations for an Enhanced Monitoring and Evaluation System for CAAHT.

Erder, Sema & Kaska, Selmin. (2003). *Irregular Migration and Trafficking in*

Women: The Case of Turkey. November 2003. International Organization for Migration: Geneva.

Fritz, Susan Kosinski. (2006). *Trafficking in Persons Assessment and Recommendations*. March 2006. USAID, Europe and Eurasia Bureau, Office of Democracy, Governance and Social Transition: Washington.

Georgian Young Lawyers Association (GYLA). (2007a). *No to Trafficking in Persons: Quarterly Report, April 1, 2007 – June 30, 2007*. Georgian Young Lawyers Association: Tblisi.

GYLA. (2007b). *No to Trafficking in Persons: Quarterly Report, January 1, 2007 – March 31, 2007*. Georgian Young Lawyers Association: Tblisi.

GYLA. (2006). *No to Trafficking in Persons: Quarterly Report, September 26, 2005 – March 31, 2006*. Georgian Young Lawyers Association: Tblisi

Ghinararu, Catalin & van der Linden, Mariska N. J. (2004). *Trafficking of Migrant Workers from Romania: Issues of Labour and Sexual Exploitation*. October 2004, Working Paper 33, International Labour Office: Geneva.

Global Alliance Against Traffic in Women (GAATW). (2007). *Collateral Damage: The Impact of Anti-Trafficking Measures on Human Rights around the World.* Global Alliance Against Traffic in Women: Bangkok.

U.S. Government Accountability Office (GAO). (2007). *Human Trafficking: Monitoring and Evaluation of International Projects are Limited, but Experts Suggest Improvements*. GAO-07-1034, United States Government Accountability Office: Washington, DC.

GAO. (2006). *Human Trafficking: Better Data, Strategy and Reporting Needed to Enhance U.S. Antitrafficking Efforts Abroad*. GAO-06-825, United States Government Accountability Office: Washington, DC.

Hampton, Ronald & Ball, Dwayne. (2008) *Preliminary Report: Key Informant Survey on Human Trafficking in Ukraine*. University of Nebraksa: Lincoln.

InterBilim. (2001). Evaluation Report of the International Organization for Migration Project: Building Capacity to Combat Trafficking if Human Beings in the Kyrgyz Republic. International Center "InterBilim": Bishkek.

International Catholic Migration Commission. (2003). *Victim Assistance and Protection Program for Women Rescued from Trafficking*. November 2003. ICMC: Croatia.

International Centre for Migration Policy Developmet. (2007). *Narrative Interim Report for the Period 30 June 2006 – 30 May 2007: Inception and Assessment Phase*. Programme to Support the Development of

Transnational Referral mechanisms for Trafficked Persons in Southeastern Europe. ICMPD: Vienna.

International Organization for Migration (IOM). (2008). Quarterly Report to USAID on Prevention of Trafficking in Persons in Belarus:, October 1 – December 31, 2007,

IOM. (2007a). Annual Report to USAID on Prevention of Trafficking in Persons in Belarus, 1 April 2006 – 31 March 2007, International Organization for Migration.

IOM. (2007b). *Combating Trafficking in Human Beings in Ukraine: Statistics Updated on 31 March 2007*. International Organization for Migration: Kyiv.

IOM. (2007c). *Micro-Enterprise Component Assessment 2007 – Report and Presentation*. International Organization for Migration: Kyiv.

IOM. (2007d). *The IOM Handbook on Direct Assistance for Victims of Trafficking*. International Organization for Migration: Geneva.

IOM. (2006a) *Annual Report to USAID on Prevention of Trafficking in Persons in Belarus*. International Organization for Migration.

IOM. (2006b). *Human Trafficking Survey: Belarus, Bulgaria, Moldova, Romania and Ukraine*. December 2006. International Organization for Migration: Kyiv.

IOM. (2006c). Interim Report to the U.S. Agency for International Development (USAID): Combating Trafficking in Persons in Central Asia. 1 October to 31 December 2005, International Organization for Migration: Almaty.

IOM. (2006d). *Final Report on IOM's Montenegro*. October 1, 2002 – March 7, 2006, International Organization for Migration: Podgorica.

IOM. (2006e). *Final Report to the United States Agency for International Development: Assistance to Victims of Trafficking in Turkey*. International Organization for Migration: Ankara.

IOM. (2005a). *Final Report on IOM's Counteries Funded by USAID Serbia*. International Organization for Migration: Belgrade.

IOM. (2005b). *Interim Report on IOM's r-Trafficking Activities Funded by USAID Serbia*. International Organization for Migration: Belgrade.

IOM. (2005c). Interim Report to the Swedish Agency for International Development (SIDA) and the U.S. Agency for International Development (USAID): Combating Trafficking in Persons in Central Asia. International Organization for Migration: Almaty; April 1 – June 30, 2005.

IOM. (2005d). *Progress Report to USAID Serbia: Program to Counteract Human Trafficking in Serbia*. International Organization for Migration:

Belgrade.

IOM. (2005e). Quarterly Report for the Period from 01 January to 31 March 2005, Appendix 2 and 3 Hotline Statistics: Combating Trafficking in Persons in Central Asia. International Organization for Migration.

IOM. (2005f). *Situation Report February 2000 to June 2005 – Return and Reintegration Project.* Counter Trafficking Unit, International Organization for Migration: Kosovo.

IOM. (2005g). Final Report: Prevention and Awareness-Raising Campaign on Trafficking in Bosnia and Herzegovina (PARC). International Organization for Migration: Sarajevo.

IOM. (2004). IOM Counter Trafficking Re-Integration to Kosovar Victims of Trafficking: January – March 2004, Project Activities and Implementation Interim Report. International Organization for Migration.

IOM. (2003). Final Report to the Swedish Agency for International Development (SIDA) and the U.S. Agency for International Development (USAID): Combating Trafficking in Human Beings From, To, Through, and Within Kazakhstan (Year II). International Organization for Migration: Almaty.

IOM. (2001). *Hardship Abroad or Hunger at Home: A Study of Irregular Migration from Georgia (Preliminary Version).* International Organization for Migration: Tblisi.

Internationl Research and Exchanges Board. (2004). Women's Programs Description.

IREX. (2003a). *Excerpt from IREX Annual Highlights*. International Research & Exchanges Board.

IREX. (2003b). Regional Empowerment Initiative for Women (REIW): Activity Highlights December – February 2003. International Research & Exchanges Board.

Kelly, Liz. (2005). *Fertile Fields: Trafficking in Persons in Central Asia.* International Organization for Migration: Vienna.

Kiryan, Tetyana & van der Linden, Mariska N. J. (2005). *Trafficking of Migrant Workers from Ukraine: Issues of Labour and Sexual Exploitation.* November 2005, Working Paper 39, International Labour Office: Geneva.

Kutnick, Bruce, Belser, Patrick & Gergana Danailova-Trainor. (2007). *Methodologies for Global and National Estimation of Human Trafficking Victims: Current and Future Approaches*. International Labour Office: Geneva.

Matei, Iana. (2005). *Report on the Assessment/Evaluation of Direct Assistance for Victims of Trafficking in Human Beings Provided by NGO OPEN*

GATE. 24 – 30 September 2005. Organization for Security and Co-operation in Europe, Spillover Monitor Mission to Skopje.

Michailov, Eduard, van der Linden, Mariska N. J. & Scanlan, Shivaun. (2005). *Forced Labour Outcomes of Migration from Moldova: Rapid Assessment*. November 2005, Working Paper 38, International Labour Office: Geneva.

MNAdvocates. (2000). *Domestic Violence in Moldova*. December 2000. Minnesota Advocates for Human Rights: Minneapolis.

Moens, Bruno. (2007). Evaluation Report on the Residence Project Implemented by Open Gate / La Strada Macedonia. October 2007, OSCE Spillover Monitoring Mission to Skopje and USAID: Skopje.

Management Systems International. (2004). *Governance and Trafficking in Persons – Georgia: Assessment, Inventory and Proposed Activities*. May 2004, Management Systems International: Washington.

Open Gate/La Strada. (2007). Residence: A Summary on the Assistance Activities in Providing Direct Assistance to Trafficking Victims in Macedonia, with a Special Focus on the Safe House for Trafficking Victims - Residence. Open Gate / La Strada Macedonia: Skopje.

Organization for Security and Co-operation in Europe. (2007). Quarterly Progress Report – February1, 2007 – April 30, 2007 – for the Residence Project. Organization for Security and Cooperation in Europe, Spillover Monitor Mission to Skopje.

Phillippe, P. & Packer, I. (2005). *Albania: Transnational Action Against Child Trafficking (TACT) Peer Revie*w. Terre des Hommes: Tirana.

Pojman, Ruth and Timoshenko, Tatiana. (2007). *Assessment of the USAID/Belarus IOM Anti-Trafficking Program*. USAID: Washington.

PRISM. (2007). *Research Study on Trafficking in Human Beings. Partnership Against Trafficking in Human Beings*. Prism Research: Kosovo.

Rosenberg, Ruth. (2006). *Shelter Assessment in Bosnia and Herzegovina*. USAID: Sarajevo.

Rosenberg, Ruth. (2004). *Best Practices for Programming to Prevent Trafficking in Human Beings in Europe and Eurasia*. Bethesda, MD: Development Alternatives, Inc. & USAID.

Saatchi & Saatchi. (2006). *Settings Reveal Regarding Working Abroad – Parts I and II*. Saatchi and Saatchi for IOM: Belarus.

Snajdrova, H. & Hanilova, B. (2007). *Trafficking in Human Beings in the Republic of Armenia*.OSCE: Yerevan.

Somach, Susan & Surtees, Rebecca. (2005). *Anti-Trafficking Technical Assistance: Albania Anti-Trafficking Evaluation October 24 – December 19, 2005*. Chemonics International Inc.: Washington.

Somach, Susan (n.d.). Assessment of IREX's Trafficking Prevention and Information Dissemination (TPID) Program. International Research & Exchanges Board (IREX)

Stefkovska – Veljanovska, Gordana. (2005). *Program Evaluation of SOS – Helpline Project of Open Gate/La Strada*. Center for Institutional Development – CITa: Skoje.

Stephens, Sarah & van der Linden, Mariska N. J. (2005). *Trafficking of Migrant Workers from Albania: Issues of Labour and Sexual Exploitation.* September 2005, Working Paper 37, International Labour Office: Geneva.

Surtees, Rebecca. (2008a). *Trafficking of Men – A Trend Less Considered: The Case of Belarus and Ukraine*. IOM Global Database Thematic Research Series Geneva: International Organization for Migration: Geneva.

Surtees, Rebecca. (2008b). Trafficked Men as Unwilling Victims. St. Antony's International Review (STAIR), Issue: *The politics of trafficking., 14(1),* 16-36.

Surtees, Rebecca. (2007a). *Handbook on Anti-Trafficking Data Collection in South-Eastern Europe: Developing Regional Criteria*. International Centre for Migration Policy Development: Vienna.

Surtees, Rebecca. (2007b*). Listening to Victims: Experiences of Identification, Return and Assistance in South-Eastern Europe*. International Centre for Migration Policy Development: Vienna.

Surtees, Rebecca. (2006). *Evaluating Anti-Trafficking Victim Assistance in Southeastern Europe: A Strategic Planning Paper for the King Baudouin Foundation*. Nexus Institute to Combat Human Trafficking: Vienna.

Surtees, Rebecca. (2005). *Second Annual Report on Victims of Trafficking in Southeastern Europe*. International Organization for Migration: Geneva.

Terre des Hommes. (2008). *TACT 3 – Quarterly Reports Nos 5 – 7. June 2007 – February 2008*. Terre des Hommes Foundation: Tirana.

TdH. (2007). *TACT 3 – Yearly Report June 2006 – June 2007*. Terre des Hommes Foundation: Tirana.

TdH. (2006). *TACT II Final report May 2003 – May 2006*. Terre des Hommes Foundation: Tirana.

TdH. (2005a). *21-Month Implementation Report TACT Donor Meeting: 1 May 03 – 28 February 05*. Terre des Hommes Foundation: Tirana.

TdH. (2005b). TACT Program Quarterly Report to USAID – No. 10: 1 September 05 – 30 November 05. Terre des Hommes Foundation: Tirana.

Thompson, Katy & Jernow, Allison. (2008). *Compensation for Trafficked and Exploited Persons in the OSCE Region*. Organization for Security and Cooperation in Europe (OSCE), Office for Democratic Institutions and

Human Rights (ODIHR): Warsaw.

Tiurukanova, Elena. (2006). *Human Trafficking in the Russian Federation: Inventory and Analysis of the Current Situation and Responses*. Institute for Urban Economics: Moscow.

Townsend, Mark. (2007, December 16). 'Sex slaves' win cash in landmark legal deal. *The Observer*, p. 1 (accessed December 2007 from http://www.guardian.co.uk/uk/2007/dec/16/immigration.ukcrime)

United Nations Development Programme. (2005). *Project Completion Report – EU/UNDP Combating Trafficking in Women n the Republic of Belarus, September 2002-November 2005*. UNDP: Minsk.

UNICEF. (2006). *Guidelines for the Protection of Child Victims of Trafficking. Provision Version 2.1, September 2006*. UNICEF: New York.

USAID. (2006). *Trafficking in Persons: USAID'sce of Women in Development,* USAID: Washington.

USAID. (2007). The Rehabilitation of Victims of Trafficking in Group Residential Facilities in Foreign Countries: A study conducted pursuant to the Trafficking Victims Protection Reauthorization Act, 2005. USAID and Chemonics International, Inc.: Washington, DC. September 2007.

Velkoska, Violeta. (2005). *Combating Trafficking in Human Beings through the Practice of the Domestic Courts*. November 2005, Coalition 'All

Warnath, Stephen. (2007). *Examining the Intersection between Trafficking in Persons and Domestic Violence*. E&E Office of Social Transition, USAID: Washington.

Watson, Charlotte. (2005a). Trafficking in Persons Assessment Kazakhstan. USAID CAR. June 2005.

Watson, Charlotte. (2005b). Trafficking in Persons Assessment Kyrgyzstan. USAID CAR. June 2005.

Watson, Charlotte. (2005c). Trafficking in Persons Assessment Tajikistan. USAID CAR. June 2005.

Watson, Charlotte. (2005d). Trafficking in Persons Assessment Uzbekistan. USAID CAR. June 2005.

Winrock. (2007). *Anti-trafficking Initiative in Moldova, New Perspectives for Women: First Quarterly Progress Report for 2007*. Winrock International.

Winrock. (2005). *Women at Risk in the Republic of Moldova: National Representative Survey*. IMAS Inc for Winrock International.

Winrock. (2004a). *Baseline Assessment – Preventing Human Trafficking in Kyrgyzstan Project*. Winrock International. March 2004.

Winrock. (2004b). *Final Report – Prevention of Trafficking in Women through Expansion of Economic Opportunities in Belarus*. Winrock International.

Winrock PMEP (n.d.) *Winrock Performance Monitoring and Evaluation Plan.* Winrock Moldova.

World Learning. (2003). *Quarterly Report of Activities: Romanian American Sustainable Partnerships (RASP) Umbrella Grant Activity.* World Learning: Bucharest.

ANNEX B. TOOL KIT FOR DESIGNING TRAFFICKING PROTECTION PROGRAMS

I. Purpose

USAID staff are often tasked with designing and managing anti-trafficking (anti-TIP) projects as one of their many other responsibilities, without having specific expertise in the area. This Tool Kit has been developed with such a person in mind and aims to help them design and implement successful programs by taking into consideration the following issues: objectives to achieve, critical issues to consider for each objective, possible interventions, expected results, and impact indicators. These programming ideas are based on lessons learned from the analysis of past and on-going anti-TIP programming in the Europe and Eurasia region.

II. Designing Protection Programs

The subsections below illustrate and discuss the key features needed in the design of a successful protection program.

Consult with Beneficiaries during the Design Phase

As with any development program it is important to consult with stakeholders when designing new projects. Thus, it is equally important to consult with the potential beneficiaries (i.e., victims of trafficking, or VoTs) of protection programs to better understand their needs and constraints. However, such consultations need to be done ethically, sensitively, and with the voluntary participation of the beneficiaries. Individuals who are designing protection programs should have experience interacting or be trained on how to interact with VoTs prior to such consultations.

Design Interventions that Encompass Neglected Targets

With anti-TIP efforts, it is important to recognize that the nature and dynamics of trafficking changes over time. Programs should be designed so that they naturally adapt to the changing dynamics and also so that capacity-building efforts are as relevant ten years after the program ends as they are after one year. In order to do this, the program must take into consideration that there is not one profile of trafficked persons. Trafficked persons can be any gender, age, religious background, or ethnicity and may have been trafficked for a wide variety of exploitative purposes. Even if such persons have not yet been identified, it is important to be cognizant when designing interventions that such patterns of trafficking can emerge. When considering which categories of persons might be vulnerable to trafficking, but not yet identified, anti-trafficking stakeholders should consider all categories of persons who are known to emigrate for work or study as well as those who work away from home or in the homes of others. They should be observant of trends emerging other countries and in their regions and consider whether those trends may be emerging in their own country.

Exit Strategy and Sustainability

International donor funding will not be available forever and in Europe and Eurasia, in particular, more and more countries are graduating from assistance. Therefore, it is important to ensure that donor-funded interventions are designed in such a way as to maximize sustainability. Issues of sustainability are discussed for every objective that follows, but some key themes that run throughout include:

- Training should be integrated into existing and ongoing training mechanisms.
- Best practices should be integrated into obligatory protocols and procedures.
- Cost-sharing from state and local governments should be encouraged.
- Local fund-raising mechanisms should be developed.

Short-Term Funding

One of the problems inherent in the design of many anti-TIP programs is their short-term nature. Expecting to achieve significant impact and sustainability of services in a short time is not realistic. Not only does short-term funding put a strain on service providers who have to spend significantly more time raising funds, but it also limits their ability to monitor the impacts of the programs and to provide continuous services for VoTs.

Too Many Partners / Sub-Grants

Too many partners with too many small grants can result in programs that are inappropriately focused and leave little time or money for capacity building or proper management and oversight of sub-grants (e.g., Watson, 2005b, p. 9). Donors should encourage partners to maintain focused programs and to build the capacity of fewer organizations, rather than trying to support all the organizations in their community or region.

Combining Prevention with (Re)Integration

Some anti-TIP efforts have combined the provision of services for vulnerable groups with those for VoTs when feasible. This has the possibility of reducing the stigma associated with trafficking by allowing trafficked persons to blend with other populations. This can also ease the victims' transition to normalized relations with the "outside" world.

This prevention-integration arrangement can be achieved by combining prevention and protection programs or by integrating trafficked persons as beneficiaries into non-trafficking programs – for example, by assisting trafficked persons to apply for micro-credit programs designed for the general population. Such integration can also be achieved by offering vocational training and employment programs as both reintegration for former victims of trafficking and prevention for groups vulnerable to being trafficked. It is important, however, that impact data be disaggregated to better assess the impact of the projects on victim protection and to help ascertain if programs need to be adapted in some way to be effective for trafficked persons.

III. Programming Objectives and Interventions

A. Identification

Programming Objective 1: *Establish and effectively implement procedures for law enforcement and border management officials for the identification and referral of victims of trafficking*

Critical Aspects of Interventions

Law enforcement officers and border officials should be given clear instructions on how to handle situations which could be indicative of trafficking. They should be trained to be sensitive to the fact that VoTs can include a wide-ranging demographic: women, men, children, and adults, ethnic minorities, foreigners, and local nationals. They should be trained to recognize the signs of exploitation and trafficking for myriad purposes. They should be clear on the definition of trafficking, understanding the broadest meaning of the term and clarifying any problems that arise due to confusion when trafficking terms are translated into local languages. They also need to be trained to respect the rights of individuals to travel and make their own informed decisions. If they suspect that a person is being coerced into crossing the border, they should interview them alone, without the presence of those who are accompanying them and try to offer them security and protection. While border guards may warn those who they believe could be in transit to becoming VoTs, they should not violate their rights in an effort to protect them.

DO NO HARM

Donors should be careful when selecting organizations to implement hotlines. It is critical, that hotlines are staffed by properly trained professionals and that these professionals have clear guidelines for how to handle calls. They are taking calls that can result in harm to themselves and others if not handled properly. In cases of rescue, there are particularly high security threats, where the lives of the victim, those around them and those assisting them can be endangered if not handled professionally. Even for prevention calls there can be unexpected harm. For example, two VOTs in Kyrgyzstan had contacted a hotline about work abroad. They were assured by the authorities to whom the were referred that the company had a license for organizing employment abroad and they were also given what appeared to be legitimate work contracts. This gave the women a false sense of security and they found themselves trafficked nonetheless. (Winrock 2004a: 31 and 32). There have also been cases of hotline operators being threatened by traffickers so that it is important that hotlines implement policies to protect the employees (Watson 2005d: 10).

Possible Interventions

- Establish procedures for law enforcement and border management officials for the identification and referral of victims of trafficking.
- Develop official instructions, handbooks, and quick reference guides.
- Develop training programs for law enforcement officers and border guards and integrate these into existing academic, pre-service, and in-service training mechanisms.

Results and Indicators

- Official instructions for law enforcement and border officials address all forms of trafficking and demographics of victims.
- There is increased identification of victims by law enforcement and border officials.
- There is increased identification of neglected target groups.
- There is an increase in referrals by law enforcement for assistance.
- Victims have fewer complaints about their treatment by law enforcement and border officials and more reports of positive treatment by law enforcement border officials.

Sustainability

Integration into existing pre- and in-service training mechanisms and formalizing effective identification mechanisms into the established operational procedures ensures sustainability.

Programming Objective 2: *Establish and make operational multi-use hotlines (for prevention purposes as well as for the identification and referral of victims of trafficking)*

Critical Aspects of Interventions

The training of hotline staff is critical to make sure they know how to handle the many types of calls that may come into the hotline. Additionally, there has been success in the E&E region with conducting co-trainings with operators of other types of hotlines in order learn from each other, but also to improve and coordinate referrals between them (OSCE 2007: Annex).

Hotline numbers need to be well advertised. Spikes in calls are noted when campaigns that include hotline numbers are underway. Other stakeholders can also be encouraged to include the hotline number in their anti-TIP campaigns (OSCE 2007: Annex).

Hotline advertisements should be well targeted to the appropriate audience, which is dependent on the type of trafficking most prevalent in any specific country. For countries of origin, this could be targeted to communities from which large numbers of immigrants originate; in destination countries, this could include clients of prostitution and immigrant communities. As well, the imagery and language used in these advertisements need to be such that the target audience will be able to identify with and/or respond to it. Use of terms such as "victim" and "trafficking" should be avoided. Alternative terms which might be considered include: persons who have been exploited, taken advantage of, had their rights violated, etc. The appropriate terms to use will obviously be dependent on the subtle meaning of terms in any particular language and culture.

Hotline numbers for countries of origin should also be accessible from overseas. Victims do try to call hotlines after leaving the country and find that they have been deceived. Calling the hotline in their country of origin may be more comfortable for them; they may be more confident of being able to speak their own language and less fearful of being arrested or deported if they have irregular status in the country to which they were trafficked. Therefore, it is useful for hotline numbers to be accessible from abroad. This does not mean, however, that these hotlines have to be free from abroad; some victims are able to access a phone and make an international call, at least briefly enough to request that someone call them back.

Possible Interventions

- Establish multi-use hotlines that can handle calls related to TIP as well as other issues.
- Provide training for hotline operators.
- Develop guidelines and manuals for hotline operators.
- Conduct targeted awareness-raising campaigns aimed at those in a position to identify VoTs (e.g., clients of prostitutes, families of migrants or recently returned migrants, etc.)

Results and Indicators

- An increased percentage of calls report possible cases of trafficking.

- In increase in the number of such calls from groups targeted for awareness-raising campaigns.
- Calls that have successful outcomes – rescue and assistance for reported victims.

Sustainability

One study of hotline services funded by USAID in Russia found that many of the hotlines had shut down shortly after donor funding ended (Somach, n.d.). Sustainability can be achieved through use of government phone lines, by linking to other emergency hotlines in the country, or through the donation of free phone service from the State or telephone company. Sustainability is also achieved through the establishment of guidelines and manuals which can be used for continued training of operators after the funding ends.

Programming Objective 3: *Establish and effectively implement procedures for consular officials (or other key authorities) for the identification and referral of victims of trafficking victims of trafficking*

Critical Aspects of Interventions

Consular officials should be given clear instructions on how to handle situations which could be indicative of trafficking, including referral of their citizens to local support services. They should be trained to be sensitive to the fact that victims of trafficking can include a wide-ranging demographic: women, men, children, adults, and ethnic minorities. They should be trained to recognize the signs of exploitation and trafficking for myriad purposes. They should be clear on the definition of trafficking, understanding the broadest meaning of the term and clarifying any problems arising due to confusing in translation of terms into local languages.

Possible Interventions

- Establish instructions/procedures for consular or embassy officials for the identification and referral of victims of trafficking.
- Provide training for consular and embassy officials.
- Develop and distribute handbooks and manuals for consular and embassy officials.

Results and Indicators

- Official instructions for consular officials address all forms of trafficking and demographics of victims.
- There is increased identification of victims by consular officials.
- There is increased identification of neglected target groups.
- Victims have fewer complaints about their treatment by consular officials and more reports of positive treatment by consular officials.

AVOIDING USE OF THE TERMS "TRAFFICKING" AND "VICTIM"

Victims of trafficking may not identify themselves as such. Many studies have pointed out the fact that those who qualify as victims of trafficking according to the UN definition do not actually see themselves in this way (Brunovskis & Surtees 2007; Surtees 2007, Surtees 2008a&b). Prevention and protection materials, which typically focus on or highlight these terms, may not be effective in reaching out to the majority of victims of trafficking, who may not identify with the terms and images used.

Sustainability

Integration into existing pre- and in-service training mechanisms and formalizing effective identification and referral mechanisms into established operational procedures ensures sustainability.

Programming Objective 4: *The general public (or target groups who are likely to be in contact with trafficked persons) are aware of mechanisms for reporting and assisting exploited persons*

Critical Aspects of Interventions

Increased awareness of assistance mechanisms available for VoTs can lead to increased reporting of this crime and the referral of victims for assistance. There are many potential target groups, including returned migrants, families of migrant workers, clients of sex workers, and others. Campaigns should be carefully designed to appeal to the target audience. Terms like "trafficking" and "victim" should be avoided as they are often either misunderstood or rejected by the target audience as not relating to them. Such awareness-raising campaigns can also be designed to reduce the shame and prejudice that former victims often experience in their communities and families. This might be done by eliminating the focus on trafficking for might be done by eliminating the focus on trafficking for prostitution and other elements that cause stigmatization in the local culture. For example, a campaign may focus instead on labor exploitation, highlighting violations such as withholding of pay, poor working conditions, or being forced to do work different than that which was promised. Campaigns should use language to describe these violations which is commonly understood by the general public.

Possible Interventions

- Conduct awareness-raising campaigns aimed at the general public targeted in such a way that they increase the identification, rescue, and referral of VoTs.
- Conduct awareness-raising campaigns aimed at the general public designed to reduce stigma and prejudice against VoTs.
- Promote awareness-raising campaigns linked to anonymous hotlines for referral of TIP cases.

Results and Indicators

- An increased percentage of calls to hotlines report possible cases of trafficking.
- There is an increase in the number of such calls from groups targeted by TIP awareness-raising campaigns.
- Calls to hotlines have successful outcomes – increases in rescue and assistance for reported victims.
- There is a decrease in the stigma and prejudice faced by VoTs.

Sustainability

Awareness-raising campaigns do not tend to be self-sustaining as they usually end when the funding is completed. However, governments may be willing to share the costs of marketing such campaigns. Indeed, there are examples of government cost-sharing through free air time on television and radio, as well as free advertising space in public spaces such as at airports, on trains and buses, etc. There may also be ways to get private businesses in the country to support such interventions, by linking awareness-raising messages to advertising for companies' products and services, but, as far as the author is aware, this has not yet been explored.

DO NO HARM

It is important for donors to understand their role in ensuring that those to whom they provide the funding have the necessary skills and experience to provide such assistance. Much harm can be inflicted unintentionally. Victims can be unnecessarily traumatized, may be at risk for suicide and are often threatened or even murdered by their traffickers. Those supporting victims are also at risk, as well as as victims' family and loved ones. It is critical, therefore, that victim assistance be undertaken only by those with the appropriate experience, and donors have a responsibility to ensure that they do not give money for such assistance to organizations who do not have the skills and experience to handle it properly.

B. Direct Assistance

Programming Objective 1*: National referral mechanism is established and operational*

Critical Aspects of Interventions

National referral mechanisms (NRMs) are important tools for formalizing the identification and referral mechanisms in a country and for promoting cooperation amongst government and nongovernmental stakeholders. However, such mechanisms can also be used to give too much authority and control to one stakeholder to the detriment of the victims it is designed to assist. To protect against this, ensure victim identification and referral mechanisms include civil society actors and do not give too much authority and responsibility to law enforcement. Ensure that services provided to victims are not conditional on victims cooperating with law enforcement. NRMs should be designed together with the development of standards for victim assistance and mechanisms for monitoring implementation.

Similarly, trans-national referral mechanisms (TRMs) can be used to support the identification, rescue and referral of foreign nationals between countries of origin, transit and destination. Such mechanisms can ensure better protection and services for victims through the establishment of standards and smoother cooperation amongst participating institutions. They may also be used to improve reporting of trafficking cases and the sharing of data which can be used to monitor trends.

Possible Interventions

- Support workshops and working groups which bring together relevant stakeholders to discuss standards for victim assistance and the establishment of NRMs/TRMs.
- Support necessary research or assessments on NRMs/TRMs.
- Support training or capacity building necessary for effective implementation of NRMs/TRMs.
- Support the development of standards and monitoring mechanisms.
- Serve as a facilitator to ensure that relevant NGOs, other service providers, and stakeholders have a seat at the table and are actively involved in the process of developing NRMs/TRMs.

Results and Indicators

- A national referral mechanism is formalized.
- A national referral mechanism is fully implemented.
- The national referral mechanism works effectively (as demonstrated through monitoring mechanisms - see below).

Sustainability

Once established, the national referral mechanism should be self sustaining if it is properly formalized. Sustainability of its usefulness will then be a matter of political will.

Programming Objective 2: *Assistance programs are in place, which are tailored to the needs of a wide range of victim populations*

Critical Aspects of Interventions

Current assistance programs are generally not designed to meet the needs of male VoTs, children, minors, victims with children, or the mentally and/or physically disabled. In fact, they often do not meet the needs of the target group they are designed to assist.

> Do not assume that most victims of trafficking are women trafficked for prostitution just because the current data seem to indicate it. Data are skewed by how they are collected.

Possible Interventions

- Support research into the needs, perceptions, and experiences with assistance of neglected TIP victim populations.
- Support assistance to a wide range of TIP victim populations.
- Develop outreach campaigns to increase identification of a wide range of TIP victim populations.

Results and Indicators

- Assistance programs for VoTs are in place, which are tailored to the needs of a wide variety of victim populations, including males, victims trafficked for labor, the disabled, children, women with children, etc.
- An increased number of male VoTs receive assistance.
- An increased number of women trafficked for labor receive assistance.
- Specific guidelines developed and adhered to that describe how to assist child VoTs because minors have special needs.
- Feedback from assisted persons indicates that the services received met their needs.

Sustainability

See below for issues of sustainability of victim services generally.

Programming Objective 3: *Providing information about assistance to potential VoTs and to VoTs upon repatriation*

Critical Aspects of Interventions

Providing information to victims of trafficking and those at risk of being victimized (migrant workers, women in prostitution, graduates of orphanages, etc.) is an important method of increasing identification and improving the provision of assistance to victims. Information needs to be designed for distribution during different phases in order to reach out to the most victims possible and to provide information as it is needed. For example, before going abroad, in order to inform potential victims of trafficking about assistance available if they should have trouble in their country of destination; upon identification and before repatriation to country of origin to provide victims with information about assistance available to them now as well as in their home country should they decide to return; and after repatriation/return in order to reach out to victims who may not have been identified. It is important to use language and designs with which the target audience can identify.

Possible Interventions

- Develop flyers to be distributed with new passports, at border crossing points and on cross-border transportation (for those departing and returning to the country). Such flyers might include information about the rights of migrants and provide information about where migrants can get help should they encounter violations of their rights (such as contact details for Embassies and consulates, hotlines, and relevant NGOs and IOs both at home and in key destination countries. As noted in Section A, the flyer should avoid terms such a trafficking and use language with which the target population may better identify (see Section A above).
- Develop information about available assistance in the language of trafficked persons for distribution by police, social workers, medical professionals, consular officials, and other people who may be in contact with VoTs in destination and transit countries. It may be necessary to emphasize that exploited (trafficked) persons will not be prosecuted for crimes committed while they were exploited (trafficked).
- Explore the use of technology for providing information to VoTs (see examples in *Best Practices in Trafficking Protection Programming*, chapter 4).

Results and Indicators

- There is an increase in the number of victims and potential victims seeking assistance because they received the materials on assistance for VoTs that were developed.

- There is an increase in the number and percentage of VoTs who report feeling more knowledgeable and comfortable about assistance as a result of the written materials.

Sustainability

Developing materials in coordination with the government will increase their likelihood of being sustained. Ensuring that the government gives instructions to border guards, police officers and other relevant officials in regard to their distribution will ensure that they are distributed as intended.

Programming Objective 4: *Victim assistance services become sustainable*

Critical Aspects of Interventions

Services need to be designed with flexibility in mind in order to adapt to the changing trafficking dynamics, while still being cost effective. Local funding sources are also needed to ensure long-term sustainability of services. These may include state and local government support and contributions from private donations and local businesses whose profits support the provision of services.

Establish oversight mechanisms to ensure that victims of trafficking are not forced to work in social businesses in exchange for assistance.

Possible Interventions

- Design and provide flexible shelter models for VoTs.
- Develop non-shelter based services for VoTs (see Objectives 5 and 6 below).
- Advocate for government and private sponsorship of services for VoTs.
- Support the development of and seed money for social businesses whose profits would support the provision of services for VoTs.

Results and Indicators

- An increasing percentage of operating expenses of shelters that provide anti-trafficking services are obtained from local resources.
- The cost of providing one night's shelter for one VoT is reduced, without reducing the quality and security of services.

- The cost of providing an overall assistance package to victims is reduced without reducing the quality and security of services.

Sustainability

Reducing costs for the provision of services while increasing local financial support leads to the financial sustainability of these services.

Programming Objective 5: *Expand victim services beyond shelters and beyond the capital cities*

Critical Aspects of Interventions

Currently most services for VoTs are linked to shelter-based mechanisms and are primarily available only in the capital cities, major urban centers, and border areas. Many victims return to their families who may live in more remote locations, but these VoTs still require reintegration assistance. Others may wish to live in the capital city, but do not need or desire to live in a shelter. Expanding the availability of services beyond those provided at shelters, as well as to more remote locations in the country, is an important aspect of making services accessible in such a way as to promote full reintegration.

Possible Interventions

- Develop service models that will extend to relevant areas of the country.
- Provide funding for assistance through these models.

Results and Indicators

- Services for VoTs are available in locations throughout the country.
- There is an increase in the number of victims accessing services from remote locations.
- There is an increase in victims' accessibility to and satisfaction with services.

Sustainability

The manner in which services are expanded will decide how sustainable they are. See Objective 6 (below) for one way of making expanded, community-based services more sustainable, by integrating them into existing social service systems.

Programming Objective 6: *Engage state social services in service provision for victims of trafficking*

Critical Aspects of Interventions

Most countries in the region have a state social service department with offices throughout the country. These offices are usually responsible for registering vulnerable groups, but VoTs may not be included in the list of groups considered "vulnerable." Revisions to laws or regulations may be needed to add VoTs to the list of eligible persons and to give responsibility to the state social services to provide them with assistance. Similarly, social workers may need training and guidance to help them understand the special needs of VoTs. In some countries, social workers may also need training to expand the scope of their work to include a more pro-active approach, one that moves beyond disbursements of social assistance to conducting outreach in their communities.

Possible Interventions

- Revise law or regulations to make VoTs eligible for social services.
- Develop handbooks and reference guides for social workers that inform these social workers and other service professionals that work with VoTs about issues specific to VoTs.
- Develop and implement training programs for social workers and other service professionals that work with victims of TIP.

Results and Indicators

- Laws and/or regulations are in place to make VoTs eligible for state-funded social services.
- Handbooks and reference guides for social workers are developed; social workers and other service professionals are aware of VoT-specific issues.
- Training programs for social workers and other service professionals are developed and integrated into existing academic, pre-service, and in-service training mechanisms.

- The number of VoTs receiving assistance from state social services increases.
- Victims have fewer complaints about their treatment by state social services and more reports of positive treatment by state social services.

Sustainability

Transferring responsibility for service provision to victims of trafficking to already established and funded state institutions makes services sustainable. Integration of training into existing academic programs and in-service training mechanisms helps to sustain specialization of services for trafficked persons.

Programming Objective 7: *Increase income generating opportunities for former victims of trafficking*

Critical Aspects of Interventions

Providing income-generating opportunities for VoTs is a critical part of any recovery program. Low income has been stated repeatedly as a push factor that increases vulnerability to the false promises of traffickers. After their escape from trafficking, VoTs are usually still in need of earning a living, either for themselves or to support their families. Assistance programs that do not address this need for income generation are not likely to succeed. Income-generating activities can begin as soon as victims feel ready, regardless of whether they are residing in shelters or not.

Possible Interventions

- Support vocational skills training for the target group, both in shelters and in the community in general.
- Develop job-seeking skills training for VoTs.
- Build the capacity of local actors to develop and support employment programs.
- Build the capacity of local actors (businesses and NGOs) to develop and support entrepreneurship programs.
- Provide seed money for cooperative businesses[20] employing VoTs or selling products made by them.

Results and Indicators

- Income earned by former victims of trafficking compares favorably to national averages.
- The percentage of VoTs who continue to earn income sufficient for their needs one year after participating in an employment or skills-related program meets an established threshold.
- TIP victims assess the income-generating intervention as having had a positive impact on their family economics and future plans.

Sustainability

Coordinating vocational training and job counseling with government-funded employment agencies would increase sustainability of services. Businesses developed with seed money should have viable business plans so that they are designed to be self-sustaining.

Programming Objective 8: *Medical services for victims of trafficking are provided by the state*

Critical Aspects of Interventions

Currently, medical services are provided primarily by international donors. This is not sustainable and does not even provide sufficient assistance to victims in the short term with chronic medical problems. Efforts to engage the state to take over the provision of medical services for VoTs are critical. Medical services need to be provided for both foreign and national VoTs.

Possible Interventions

- Reform the country's health insurance schemes to include VoTs as eligible for free medical services. The duration of eligibility should be determined on an individual basis, taking into account the structure of benefits and services available within the country's health care system, as well as the prospects of the VoT finding work.
- Advocate for government funding of medical services to VoTs.

Results and Indicators

- VoTs are included in free medical care schemes of the state.

- There is an increase in the percentage of a TIP victim's medical expenses that are covered by the state.

Sustainability

By enrolling VoTs in state health insurance schemes, provision of medical services to victims becomes sustainable.

Programming Objective 9: *Increased capacity of social workers to provide assistance to victims of trafficking*

Critical Aspects of Interventions

A lack of professional training for staff providing assistance to victims has been noted in the region (Somach & Surtees, 2005). Training and study tours for staff providing direct assistance to victims have been key components of several anti-TIP projects in the region and have included such topics as stress management and burn-out, functioning of referral systems, job development skills, entrepreneurship training, legal and mental health assistance to trafficked persons, among others (IOM, 2005a, p. 11; IOM, 2005c, p. 17; IOM, 2006a, p. 6-8; IOM, 2007a, p. 3-5). Such training activities are useful, but do not have lasting impact unless the knowledge gained can be integrated into existing academic programs and in-service training mechanisms for social workers. Future training efforts should be implemented through such sustainable mechanisms.

Possible Interventions

- Conduct a training needs assessment for social service professionals who work with VoTs.
- Provide training to professors of social work on relevant topics related to assisting VoTs.
- Develop specialized courses on TIP for schools of social work.
- Develop specialized courses on TIP for in-service training for current social workers.
- Organize study tours for social workers to countries and organizations that provide exemplary services for VoTs.

Results and Indicators

- Schools of social work offer specialized courses relevant for assisting trafficking victims.
- In-service programs are available for existing social workers that cover the special needs of trafficked persons.
- Victims report receiving improved services from social workers.

Sustainability

Integration of training into existing academic programs and in-service training mechanisms helps to sustain specialization of services for trafficked persons.

Programming Objective 10: *Improved regulation and monitoring of services to victims of trafficking*

Critical Aspects of Interventions

Currently, services are primarily provided to VoTs from NGOs. There is, in most countries of the region, little oversight of these NGOs. In many countries, there are no established standards, no licensing procedures, and no oversight of their operations. To prevent neglect, mistreatment, and abuse, as well as to ensure that the services that are provided are of high quality, it is necessary to establish oversight mechanisms.

Possible Interventions

- Develop standards of assistance for different populations of TIP victims.
- Establish licensing procedures for providers of services to TIP victims.
- Establish monitoring and evaluation mechanisms by which service providers to TIP victims obtain and maintain licenses.
- Establish clear guidelines as to what government body will be responsible for issues related to licensing and monitoring organizations that provide services to TIP victims.

Results and Indicators

- There are improved standards of assistance for VoTs.
- Treatment of VoTs by all elements of the identification and referral mechanisms meets the standards of assistance that have been established.
- Higher percentages of VoTs report positive (i.e., high quality) treatment by service providers.

Sustainability

An oversight and monitoring mechanism can be made sustainable if incorporated into the legislative and policy framework of a country. By integrating regulation with licensing procedures, the state takes responsibility for this mechanism's continued operation and oversight.

C. Legal Proceedings

Programming Objective 1: *Reduce impacts of testifying on victims*

Critical Aspects of Interventions

Participation in criminal trials can be very demanding and have severe negative impacts on VoTs. Trials tend to be very lengthy, often dragging on for years, while the victim remains in "protective custody," restricted to life in a shelter and unable to begin the transition to normalcy. Also, victims are often forced to confront their trafficker, both formally in the courtroom and often informally, and with fewer protections, in the courthouse waiting to be called for testimony.

Possible Interventions

- Ensure that the law allows for alternative mechanisms of testifying in court cases, alternatives that protect victims from confronting their traffickers and also allow victims to return to their country of origin as soon as possible – either filming their testimony in advance, providing for video-linked testimony from their country of residence, or bringing victims back in time to testify.

- Increase efforts to put these mechanisms in use. Such efforts include the training of victim advocates, prosecutors and judges and the development of bench books, quick reference guides, etc.
- Ensure that victims are provided with legal representatives who can ensure that they benefit from such protective measures.

Results and Indicators

- Laws allow for alternative mechanisms for testifying against traffickers which reduce the negative impact of testifying on VoTs.
- There is increased use of such alternative mechanisms for testifying in trafficking trials.
- VoTs spend less time in closed shelters awaiting trials.
- More VoTs are willing to testify against their traffickers because of increased safety measures and decreased discomfort.

Sustainability

By legislating changes, the possibility for alternative forms of providing testimony becomes law and, therefore, sustainable. By encouraging the use of the legislative changes, legal personnel will becoming familiar with them, will see their benefit, and will apply them more frequently.

Programming Objective 2: *Increased protection of victim identity*

Critical Aspects of Interventions

In many countries there are no laws to protect victims from having their identity exposed in the media. Revealing victims' identity publicly can have many negative consequences, anything from increasing their shame and making it more difficult to reintegrate into society to putting victims (or their family and associates) at risk from their traffickers. Furthermore, revealing victims' identities can result in victims refusing to cooperate further with law enforcement or to access assistance services.

Possible Interventions

- Enact laws which make it illegal for media outlets to expose TIP victims' identities.

- Incorporate the importance of protecting the identity of TIP victims into training for journalists.
- Assist journalists' association(s) in developing a code of conduct that would protect TIP victim identity.
- Enact laws which require authorities to protect TIP victims from media exposure.
- Enact laws that allow judges to restrict the public and media from trafficking trials.
- Pursue legal cases where media has broken the TIP victim protection laws.

Results and Indicators

- Laws are in place to protect TIP victims' identity.
- There is a significant reduction in the number of cases in which a TIP victim's name, address, photo, or other identifying information is revealed publicly.

Sustainability

By legislating changes, victim protection should be sustainable. By encouraging the use of the legislative changes through training, development of ethical codes, and pursuit of legal cases where the laws were broken, application of the law will be encouraged.

Programming Objective 3: *Ensure victims of trafficking receive amnesty for crimes committed while trafficked*

Critical Aspects of Interventions

A lack of amnesty for victims against being charged for crimes committed while trafficked may prevent victims from coming forward to testify. In some countries, it is also considered a crime for a witness not to testify, thereby requiring by law that VoTs cooperate with law enforcement and testify against their traffickers. As a result of such laws, some victims have been arrested for withdrawing a complaint of trafficking after being threatened by the traffickers.

Possible Interventions

- Ensure that laws allow amnesty for crimes committed while a VoT was trafficked.
- Ensure that the laws do not allow for VoTs to be arrested for refusing to testify.
- Ensure that VoTs are provided with legal representatives who can ensure that their rights are protected.
- Provide training for police, prosecutors, and victim advocates on protecting VoTs.

Results and Indicators

- Laws are in place to provide victims with amnesty for crimes that were committed while they were trafficked.
- Laws are not in place that allow VoTs to be arrested for refusing to testify against their traffickers.
- There is a reduction in the number of cases of VoTs being arrested for crimes committed while they were trafficked.
- There is a reduction in the number of VoTs reporting being threatened with arrest for crimes committed while they were trafficked.

Sustainability

Legislation should be sustainable. By encouraging the use of the legislative changes through training of legal enforcers, familiarity with the law will increase and will, in turn, generate sustainability.

Programming Objective 4: *Increase the amount of compensation awarded to victims of trafficking and the frequency of victims being awarded such compensation*

Critical Aspects of Interventions

Awarding compensation to victims is critical. Not only will the possibility of receiving compensation be an incentive for victims to testify against traffickers, but it also eases their reintegration, empowers the victim, and relieves the state of some of the cost of rehabilitation (when compensation is paid by the trafficker), as the victim will have access to funds to assist in his/her own recovery – paying for further education, starting a small business, etc. There are several ways in which victims are awarded compensation: through criminal proceedings, civil courts, victim compensation funds (funds set up and paid out by the State or local governments), and administrative procedures and mediated settlements. The seizure of trafficker's assets is critical to ensuring that funds are available to pay compensation awarded by the court.

Possible Interventions

- Initiate legal analysis and reform to allow for the following:
  - Confiscation of traffickers' assets to pay compensation to victims;
  - Allowing claims for compensation within the criminal proceedings related to TIP cases, either through the prosecutor or by the VoT;
  - Improved procedures for implementation of court awarded damages or compensation claims to VoTs;
  - Development of state-supported victim compensation funds (the funding for which can be provided by the State as well as by fines and penalties imposed on traffickers).
  - Strengthening administrative procedures that award compensation to VoTs, such as through labor inspectorates or equal opportunity bodies.
- Build the capacity of relevant actors to award compensation.
- Develop and distribute handbooks and manuals for prosecutors, judges and attorneys that inform them about TIP.
- Support organizations providing legal assistance to victim-witnesses, especially as related to compensation issues.

Results and Indicators

- Laws are in place that provide mechanisms for compensation to VoTs.
- An increased number of court cases results in awards of compensation to VoTs.
- An increased amount of financial compensation is awarded to VoTs.
- Payment rates of awarded compensation to VoTs improve.

Sustainability

Legislation should be sustainable. By encouraging the use of the legislative changes through training of legal enforcers, familiarity with the law will bring sustainability.

D. Quantifying Trafficking

Programming Objective 1: *More research on prevalence rates*

Critical Aspects of Interventions

The ultimate objective of anti-TIP efforts is to reduce the occurrence of TIP and the number of people trafficked. Therefore, analyzing the impact of such efforts necessarily requires that one is able to estimate the number of VoTs. Research can also be used to contradict popular myths that could lead to more people being trafficked because they believe these falsehoods and are unaware of the true dynamics of trafficking (Watson, 2005d, p. 8). Research can also be used to influence government action, especially if the government has been unwilling to recognize the issue of trafficking and the research makes a compelling case that it is a significant problem. A number of promising methodologies have been developed for quantifying the prevalence of trafficking (see *Best Practices in Trafficking Protection Programming*, chapter 4). Donors should carefully select implementing organizations that have the necessary experience to design and implement the research, otherwise the findings may not be reliable or informative.

Possible Interventions

- Design and conduct research on the prevalence of TIP.
- Provide training for local researchers in designing and conducting such research.

Results and Indicators

- Prevalence data are available and reliable.

Sustainability

Sustainability could be achieved by working with national statistics offices to incorporate trafficking related questions into existing surveys of the population, such as labor force surveys, demographic and health surveys, census studies, etc.

IV. MONITORING AND EVALUATION

The importance of monitoring and evaluation (M&E) cannot be overstated. M&E of anti-TIP programs is not only important for USAID to understand the impact of projects it funds; it is also important to ensure that assistance provided to victims is safe, effective, and does not harm victims rather than assist them. For all donors, it is important that the desired results are clearly articulated and that there are clear indicators in place to measure success. For implementing organizations, as well, it is important to use monitoring to measure their program impact and adjust programs as necessary. There has been a lack of adequate M&E in nearly all of the protection programs reviewed for this chapter.

There are many difficulties involved in assessing the impact of protection programs, especially when it comes to direct assistance for VoTs. One difficulty is determining how "success" is defined, and the other is the time frame in which this success is measured.

Defining Long-Term Success

There are some studies that have shown that VoTs and those providing assistance to them may have different definitions of successful (re)integration. For example, assistance providers may define success as the victim not attempting to migrate again (Brunovskis & Surtees, 2007),while the victim may define success as migrating, finding a good job abroad, and being able to send money home. Researchers have found that, in general, returned migrants, including VoTs, wished to work abroad again, regardless of their trafficking experiences the first time around – which often included violence and many other human rights abuses. In Ukraine, 60 percent of trafficked persons wished to go abroad again, while in Romania and Albania some 78 percent and 93 percent, respectively, wanted to migrate again (Kiryan & van der Linden,

2005, p. 42; Ghinararu & van der Linden, 2004, p. 42; Stephens & van der Linden, 2005, p. 34). Therefore, defining what is meant by success for direct assistance programs can be very difficult.

Assessing Success: Time Frame

There is a need to follow-up with beneficiaries to see how they benefited from the services provided. Different programs use different time frames to measure success of reintegration, anywhere from as few as three months to as much as three years (Somach & Surtees, 2005). Longer time frames are able to demonstrate more impact, but are complicated by the length of donor funding as well as the implementing organization's ability to maintain contact with the victims, who may have moved, changed telephone numbers, married and changed their name, or simply do not wish to be contacted.

These difficulties notwithstanding, developing impact indicators is critical and these indicators need to be qualitative as well as quantitative. For example, it is not enough that victims are identified; implementing organizations should also measure how they are treated at identification in order to ensure that those who are identifying victims do not further violate their rights and ensure that victims are referred for services. Similarly, it is not enough to measure that a VoT obtained employment. How the VoT perceives the job and whether or not the income is sufficient for his/her needs and aspirations also needs to be measured. Therefore, qualitative as well as quantitative indicators are included throughout the M&E of anti-TIP programming.

This Tool Kit is not intended to be a how to manual for the provision of direct assistance to victims of trafficking. Many resources are already available which provide guidelines for service providers; see especially:

- *The IOM Handbook on Direct Assistance for Victims of Trafficking* (IOM, 2007d).
- Anti-Slavery International's *Protocol for Identification and Assistance to Trafficked Persons and Training Kit* (2005).
- UNICEF's *Guidelines for the Protection of Child Victims of Trafficking* (2006).
- ILO's *Psycho-Social Rehabilitation of Children Withdrawn from Trafficking and Other Worst Forms of Child Labour* (2007).

- USAID and International Centre for Migration Policy Development's *Listening to Victims* (2007).

End Notes

[1] For simplicity of language Bosnia and Herzegovina will henceforth be referred to as Bosnia.

[2] This chapter is not intended to be a how-to guide for those providing direct assistance to victims of trafficking. Many excellent resources are already available which provide guidelines for direct service providers; see especially *The IOM Handbook on Direct Assistance for Victims of Trafficking* (IOM 2007d), Anti-Slavery International's *Protocol for Identification and Assistance to Trafficked Persons and Training Kit* (2005), as well as UNICEF's *Guidelines for the Protection of Child Victims of Trafficking* (UNICEF 2006).

[3] From the author's interviews with Albania anti-trafficking stakeholders, June 2008.

[4] While it is useful for hotline numbers to be accessible from abroad, they do not have to be free from abroad, as there are many examples of victims finding ways to contact hotlines back home while abroad. There is one example of a free international hotline developed in Russia. The number is valid in several European countries of destination as well as a separate number for the United States. The cost effectiveness of such a system is not clear. Over the years, the number of calls to these hotlines has been minimal. Between 2004 and 2007 there were 8,816 calls to national hotline and only 112 calls to the international numbers. However, it is not known how many of the calls to the international numbers resulted in identification and assistance to victims of trafficking since detailed call statistics to these numbers were not available. Nor is it clear how many of those callers might not have been able to access the national hotline in Russia had the international number not been available (Angel Coalition website, http://www.angelcoalition.org/eng/call-statistics.htm, accessed on April 27, 2008).

[5] From the author's personal experience as manager of a counter-trafficking program in Mongolia.

[6] From the author's personal experience as manager ofcounter-trafficking programs in Albania.

[7] Such reductions may be due to a reduction in human trafficking per se, but could equally be due to reduced efforts to identify victims, such as conducting fewer brothel raids or paying less attention to citizens returning home –especially those returning via deportation or other irregular means.

[8] Income generating programs are not only relevant for victims of trafficking, but for the families of victims too, especially the families of child victims of trafficking in order to increase the total family income thereby decreasing the reliance on income from the children.

[9] The report from this program shows that those VOTs who participated in the training program but whose business plans were not funded, all still found gainful employment (IOM 2007c).

[10] Interview with staff and beneficiary from Different and Equal NGO, Tirana, Albania (May 2008).

[11] From the author's personal experience as manager of counter trafficking programs in Albania.

[12] Ibid.

[13] Note however, that some countries have established standards for social services generally or for residential facilities, especially those housing children, but not specifically for those catering to victims of trafficking.

[14] Ibid.

[15] Ibid.

[16] In Ukraine, some courts have denied or lowered compensation claims because the victim's recruitment into prostitution had been voluntary.

[17] Many victims do not return to their country of origin after identification as a VOT or may return without notification to authorities or assistance providers in their countries of origin. According to the Dutch Rapporteur's report, most victims of trafficking are not provided with legal residency in the Netherlands. Therefore they are staying illegally, going to a third country or returning home without assistance (Dettmeijer-Vermeulen et al., 2008).

[18] Note that the RCP attempted to obtain victim data from destination countries but had great difficulty in doing so (Surtees, 2005, p.26)

[19] There is also the question of whether or not victims in destination countries have their nationalities correctly reported. Many victims travel under false identities and may maintain these false identities even after being rescued and assisted. For example, given the current easing of travel restrictions for Bulgarian and Romanian citizens into the EU at this time, it is quite possible that many migrants and victims of trafficking travel under false identities as Bulgarians or Romanians in order to facilitate their entry into the EU, with the result that the data from their actual country of origin would be underreported.

[20] The term 'cooperative business' is used here to refer to a form of social business who's profits are divided amongst those whom it is deigned to support and who contribute directly to the business. For example, a business through which the handicrafts of former victims of trafficking are sold, the profits from which are given directly to those who made the handicrafts.

INDEX

T